FUSION OF CULTURES

The Spirit of ArgyllAmerica Revealed

ERNEST R. GILCHRIST

BRAND *Ideas*™
Publications

Atlanta

BRANDideas™ Publications
5805 State Bridge Rd.
Suite G-274
Johns Creek, GA 30097

LCCN: 2011935320
ISBN-13: 978-0-615-51960-9
ISBN-10: 0615519601

Photography by Ernest R. Gilchrist, unless otherwise noted.
Cover Design by Michael Angelo Chester
Book Interior Design and Layout by Lady Dragonfly Publishing, LLC

Printed in the United States of America.

First Edition

10 9 8 7 6 5 4 3 2 1

To my wife,

Synetha

Whose endearing love, sacrifice and support

helped sustain me during this journey.

And our children,

Darius & Tamara

Always remember to "pray, meditate and

see yourself being successful"

Contents

FOREWORD

ERNEST R. GILCHRIST charts a vision in *Fusion of Cultures: The Spirit of ArgyllAmerica Revealed*. Beginning from his birthplace in North Carolina's Cape Fear Region, he shapes memoir and history; drawing on the Old Stories we live our lives by. Rooting imagination and memory in slavery, the Market House in Fayetteville, North Carolina, he offers the promise that the 21st century may present the many cultures of people working together, getting along with decency and respect for one another.

Gilchrist connects his home-country, his beloved Cameron Hill, with his roots in West Africa. And he feels a spiritual kinship with Paul Green, North Carolina's Dramatist Laureate, who was born, 1894, in Harnett County, near Lillington, not many miles from Gilchrist's home in Johnsonville. On Broadway, 1927, with an all-black cast, Green's *In Abraham's Bosom* won a Pulitzer Prize. The dramatist's themes settle like rivulets throughout Gilchrist's *Fusion of Cultures: The Spirit of ArgyllAmerica Revealed*, especially the notion that Society can commit no sin greater than denying an individual the right of fulfillment.

Gilchrist tells his "all-American" story from his head and heart: he gets a scholarship to play basketball at Campbell College (now Campbell University), Buies Creek, North Carolina. That was thirty-five years ago. Ernest Gilchrist was a student in my English class. *Fusion of Cultures* continues the spirit and energy I sensed in his life and work as a student. His book presents a plentiful start to new discoveries he no doubt will pursue, just as he presents his "Campbell" story within the context of the University, founded originally in 1887 as Buies Creek Academy.

Gilchrist writes of working the fields in the Sandhills in summer, barning tobacco, priming the green leaves early morning in the dew, into the afternoon sun, a job about as close to hell as heaven allows, for there's always the Pepsi-and-nab-break, mid-morning, when the primers and fieldhands pause for that dream-like respite from labor. And he likens the Atlantic Coast Conference and his basketball career to Erskine Caldwell's *Tobacco Road*, the journey down roads and rows, out and back, the way out to a present the future holds in a return to his West African forebears, the Bubi of Equatorial Guinea's Bioko Island and the Tikar of Cameroon.

The writer takes the reader to Pinehurst and Southern Pines, North Carolina, two towns which form the hub of the Sandhills. He accounts for the origins of the region, populated and popularized by the wealthy, searching for a place of good climate and health. James Boyd's family embodies the Sandhills Story, Boyd coming to Southern Pines from Pennsylvania for the good air, raising a family in Southern Pines.

James Boyd (1888-1944) commented in letters he wrote in 1913 how he loved the "solitude without loneliness" in the Sandhills. He had been visiting his grandfather's farm in Moore County. After he contracted a mild case of infantile paralysis in the summer of 1914, he began to spend even more time in the Sandhills. By 1920, he would leave his birthplace in Harrisburg, Pennsylvania, to settle permanently in Southern Pines, which he called "the most beautiful country I know." Boyd opened his house to writers of the time, including Thomas Wolfe, F. Scott Fitzgerald, Paul Green, and Sherwood Anderson, writing his historical novels for Scribner's, his widow leaving grounds and house to the community. The James Boyd house today is called Weymouth Center. Open to lectures, concerts, poetry readings, and tours, Weymouth shines close to Weymouth Woods, well-known for the virgin longleaf pine and the endangered red-cockaded woodpecker.

Gilchrist's childhood reverberates throughout his book, as he recounts his pleasure in hearing the huge military cargo planes going over his boyhood home. That sound, too, roots his memory and recall and proportions his yearning for even greater change the currents course now in multi-felicities at Fort Bragg, North Carolina.

The most memorable part of Ernest Gilchrist's book comes for me when Gilchrist as a young man is told by his father that he has ancestors who lie buried among unmarked graves in "the white-owned Cameron Hill Presbyterian cemetery." In my mind, I can picture Ernest's father gesturing as he tells him about the "black section." He acknowledges the grave of Royal Gilchrist, the father's father. Then Ernest Gilchrist's father lifts his hand toward the direction of his grandfather's grave, as if actually walking the cemetery. In this fashion of ritual, Ernest Gilchrist, years before ever visiting, meets his grandfather and great-grandfather.

We listen to the story, I imagine, as we take our history like medicine and wait, for we know we cannot own each other or the places where we live or where we travel, let alone those spots where we may be buried or the *What* our flesh turns into.

Fusion of Cultures: The Spirit of ArgyllAmerica Revealed confronts the past, much of it heart-rending. The author envisions a life within his vow that cultures may stay and pray together, sing and dance, too, appreciating myths old and new. His exploration will not go away any time soon.

Ernest Gilchrist will not forget, either, I am certain, and the rest of the world can dance to his goodwill grounded immensely in other stories, journeys.

Shelby Stephenson

ACKNOWLEDGMENTS

This book resulted from a lifelong passion to write and for my love of research, nurtured during my enrollment in Mercer University's Executive MBA program. It also came about because of the love I have for my native North Carolina, especially the Sandhills region of the Upper Cape Fear River Valley and its unique multicultural heritage. I must thank Annie Hunt Burris, past president of the Georgia Economic Developers Association (GEDA), for once sharing a simple story about an apple and how two people, in different communities in an apple growing region of the same state, applied its use very differently; one prospered and the other did not. The city of Irving, Texas, and the beautiful Las Colinas district, where I lived for several months in 2006, was of major influence with its rich history. I was inspired by its branding, its consistent look, and the story of its origins. This, and Burris' story of the apple, motivated me to begin my research on my own history and the cultural branding of hybrid ArgyllAmerica. My wife Synetha sacrificed so much as she patiently and lovingly supported this book project. Our children, Darius and Tamara, and our nephew Darrell were especially encouraging. My "little brother" Herbert was there for me throughout the entire project and accompanied me on many research trips as we traveled *Home To My Valley* to North Carolina. Sisters Dr. Clara G. Abron, Cheryl Gilchrist, and Dr. Loretta G. Woodard, brothers Harold Gilchrist and Warren Gilchrist, and late Uncle LeeRoy Gilchrist provided support or key information. Dr. Judith Jackson, Brinkley - Clark family historian, patiently told me about our roots in America and provided her book, which she spent decades of her life researching. *Fusion of Cultures* honors the memory of my beloved brother, teammate, classmate, and friend – Carlton Thompson (RIP). Dr. Eugene Walker shared his wisdom and told me to make sure I tell the story of our resilient forebears. Michael D. Williams' counsel and inspirational words and scriptures have benefited me. Dr. William Flippin, Vaughn Irons, Richard Cox, Michael Sidberry, Randy Johnson, and Leonardo McClarty provided moral support. Thanks to my small town native South Carolinian friends, William "Zack" Cooper and James Youngs, who felt "the connection" to ArgyllAmerica after reading *Tobacco Road* – an experience they had lived. That confirmed I was on the right track. Joyce Farrar Rosemon, an established author, provided critical feedback early in the project. Thanks to her husband and my very close friend Tillmon Rosemon for giving me the book *Putting Your Passion Into Print*. Priceless! I appreciate Bismarck Appiah-Kubi for his unwavering confidence in me. He is my "symbiosis brother – twins from different mothers." Antonio Allen's music ministry has inspired me; while listening to his CD, *The Air I Breathe*, I developed the intro for my Sandhills chapter. Samuel "David" Morris, of Sammiches N' Stuff, in whose restaurant I comfortably worked during many a lunch hour, deserves my thanks. David referred me to Dale Burgess, who referred me to my editor and to Jack Sturrup III and Chaun Archer with Lady Dragonfly Publishing & Author Services. Jack and Chaun were instrumental as a partner in the *Fusion of Cultures* book project, book interior design, design of engaging websites, creative logos and ideas. Larry Small, my friend since our Mercer EMBA days, worked with me on marketing aspects and book proposals. Pamela Burks, whose consulting skills kept me organized, played an integral role in improving overall quality.

Cousin Carol Frye Henry of Jackson Hamlet, North Carolina, a leader in the Moore County community, provided valuable information about her grandfather and my great uncle, Herbert Frye. The Honorable Michael Thurmond inspired me in our brief talk at the 100 Black Men of DeKalb event in 2008, removing the mystique of writing by describing it very simply. Mamie Ellis, a colleague, showed me a beautifully designed book in which she was one of many quilters featured, and it led to my introduction to a terrific graphic artist and designer, Michael Angelo Chester. William A. "Bill" Johnson, Esq., at the time of our first meeting, was one decade shy of being a centenarian. The nephew of Paul Green, he generously shared his valuable time with me as we ate lunch, talked about his family's history, and toured his maternal family's property and grave sites in Lillington, Buies Creek, North Carolina, and in Neill's Creek Township. Laurence Avery's support and guidance was instrumental in helping me to see Paul Green at a more multi-dimensional level. The staff at the Southern Historical Collection at The Wilson Library, UNC-Chapel Hill was very helpful. Willie "Cookie" King enabled me to fact check my notes for the Overhills chapter. Cristina Lewis was just wonderful as she helped to proof the book's index at a time that I was literally "running on fumes". Monica Thurman deserves a big shout out for allowing the kids to use her dining room when Elijah tutored them. It was there, waiting in her Afro-centrically designed den, that I discovered my African heritage – my true identity going back to the Mother Land. Dr. Michael Newton, a unique leading Celtic scholar, has been a major resource to me as I uncovered the *Fusion of Cultures*. Our paths crossing is validation that I was on to something. My love of writing was fostered by the late Bonnie Cameron Gilchrist. I am forever grateful for her teaching me English and journalism in high school and for instilling in me a life-long love for the craft which I am now applying. Lieutenant Colonel Willie Collins' 15-minute conversation with me about the United States military provided a perspective that perhaps no book could convey. As for Shelby Stephenson – I didn't know that I could reach back nearly 35 years and find a friend. God placed me in his freshman English class at Campbell for a reason. He has been a true partner, aiding me in this literary journey. Stan Williamson and Tony Delp's cooperation and generous hospitality on behalf of Campbell University and its Athletics Department gave me a great opportunity to reminisce about my days as a Fighting Camel. Fred Davis, a fellow Campbell alum, high school coach, and longtime friend, offered input as I developed the Campbell story. I will always be thankful for what he and Marilyn have meant in my life. Coach Danny Roberts, who believed in me many years ago and led us to the NAIA National Championship Game, an experience of a lifetime, helped me recall that special basketball season. He and Mrs. Roberts always welcomed me to their home. Campbell University's friendly library staff helped uncover key materials and books, adding new insights to share. DeKalb County, Georgia Public Library, especially the Decatur and Wesley Chapel branches, played vital roles in helping me obtain books within and outside of their system. Dr. Kenneth L. Eastman and the Rockdale County Green Public Library staff are to be commended for their assistance, as I spent many hours writing and researching there. Kaye Lund, of the Tufts Archives at Pinehurst, turned my research trip into a wonderful experience with her professionalism, kindness, and service. The Mercer University Swilley Library's staff was truly exceptional. Kim Hyre, a Weymouth Woods park ranger, was very patient and generous that late Friday afternoon of January 29, 2010, when I showed up expecting a tour, hours before a major winter storm hit. Reverend Dr. Cynthia L. Hale, Senior Pastor of Ray of Hope Christian Church, in Decatur, Georgia, provides an excellent example of religious leadership by creating a holistic spiritual environment, reaching

God's people through preaching, teaching, and musical worship and the arts. It was often while receiving the blessings of this ministry that many of my greatest thoughts for this book occurred. I'd like to thank President Barrack Hussein Obama, for his leadership and example that one can use creative talents for tangible benefit. I have accepted his challenge to pursue excellence and self-development to create a better me and thereby contribute to redeveloping a stronger nation. Jeff Newton, my consistent friend and former Fighting Camels teammate, was instrumental in my fact checking process for that long remembered national championship runner-up season. Years ago, Jeff gave me Pat Conroy's bestselling novel *My Losing Season*, and I couldn't figure out why that particular book. Now I know. I appreciate John and Vicky Wilbourne for their friendship through the years and wonderful hospitality. John was instrumental in arranging my introduction and first meeting with Bill Johnson, a tremendous half-day experience. Kelli, the friendly employee at African Ancestry, Inc., was very helpful as I contemplated whether to order a DNA kit. I must recognize the friendly, hospitable employees at the Subway® on East Ponce de Leon Avenue in downtown Decatur, Georgia, where a significant part of the book was written and researched during my lunch hour. President Jerry M. Wallace, Vice President for Institutional Advancement Dr. Jack Britt and philanthropist Mr. Ed Gore, Sr. are appreciated for their welcoming spirit as they allowed me to enjoy the 2010 Belmont University men's basketball game in the president's suite with them. Kevin Lyle's dad from Virginia and I talked for more than an hour the weekend of the Jacksonville University men's basketball game in 2009. In that enjoyable conversation, I was able to verify facts about his son for the Campbell chapter. Dr. Delores P. Aldridge offered valuable qualified support along the way. My decades' long friend Charles "Just B Natural" Butler came through in providing music research. I thank Jimmy Stowe for helping me fact check. Tim McNeill, my life-long friend and school classmate, who has always been a leader, willingly contributed to the project. And lastly, many thanks to Mary Whyte, my editor, who "whipped" me into shape and challenged my thinking to develop a better product, which I hope the reader will enjoy.

And to any whose names do not appear here, know that some thanks are written only in the heart.

Introduction

My surname is Gilchrist (*Gille Criosd*), which is Scottish Gaelic, an ancient Celtic tongue. Its roots are Old English, meaning *Servant of Christ*. However, my ancestors are not from a lineage of kilt-wearing *Legion of Restless Men*, but they would become influenced by them – and vice versa.

Before coming to America, the ancient Celts, or pre-Scots, roamed Europe and Asia and left an impact on many cultures. Settlers in a new land across the Atlantic, these men and women were possessed with an insatiable determination to explore the untamed.

The *Thistle*, the most notable immigrant ship to bring Highlanders from Argyllshire, Scotland, to the shores of eastern North Carolina, landed in Wilmington in 1739. The Argyll Colony, also known as the Highland Cape Fear Settlement, was formed 90 miles inland, and represented one thread of Gaelic culture that would affect the hybrid character of the region. ArgyllAmerica is a dually defined hybrid originated by the author that focuses on the multicultural relationships developed by the various peoples of the region.

Mine is the real-life story of ArgyllAmerica through my lens and the written expression of the spirit manifested within me and evidenced through the actions of others, past and present. ArgyllAmerica respects the legacy of the Argyll Colony of North Carolina, yet is inclusive; embracing the reality of other cultures that co-exist in a land we know and love as America.

Yes, ArgyllAmerica is not just a place. It is a spirit. It is the fusion of cultures that pursues or seeks racial harmony, resiliency, and sustainability, and whose origins were developed in the Upper Cape Fear River Valley. In this region, along with the river valley, the longleaf pine and the Sandhills are of natural and historical significance.

The ArgyllAmerica spirit captures shared experiences, spanning several centuries and documented through religion, sports, industry, books, clothing, language, song, poetry, etc. by empirical and non-scholarly sources. Today, the Spirit of ArgyllAmerica has moved beyond its physical borders and into the regional, national, and international realm.

The spirit is not ghostly or something to be feared. To the contrary! ArgyllAmerica reveals a comprehensive spirit. It is what Indian spiritual author R.M. Duraisamy calls *atman* – the living animating core within each of us which drives everything we think, do, and say. The purpose of ArgyllAmerica is not desirous of a religious spiritual movement. Nevertheless, as a Christian, I hope that the reader will be forever blessed.

Although places are important in defining its character, ArgyllAmerica is bigger than place. The Argyll Colony story begins with the emigration of settlers from Argyll, Scotland, who made the Upper Cape Fear River Valley or the Cross Creek region of North Carolina, now greater Fayetteville, home. The Argyll Colony's name is derived from the 18th century reference to the Scottish Highlanders who settled there. Immigrants fled Scotland because of religious persecution, taxation, and poverty. What made and still makes the Argyll Colony distinctive? The principles or values of the people in this place make them culturally unique. Before arriving in America, the immigrants were geographically isolated, located in the Highlands of southwestern Scotland. Because many also isolated themselves from people in early American cities, spoke a language not many knew, called Gaelic, had an ambiguous relationship with the King of England, and were agrarians, it affected their assimilation to mainstream life.

The ArgyllAmerica I know espouses the goals of sustainable living. Many of the original immigrants communed with nature and, as many were farmers, had a keen appreciation for the soil and water, especially the Cape Fear River and its many tributaries. Paul Green, a famous Harnett County native, shed light on this relationship in his works (Paul Green, *Home to My Valley*).

*Cape Fear River from the Overlook at
Raven Rock State Park, Lillington, NC*

For several centuries, much of the Argyll Colony remained an agrarian society, comparable to the life most Highlanders lived in Scotland. African slaves, many of whom entered at Brunswick and later Wilmington, were sold at, among other places, the Market House in nearby Fayetteville, or migrated from Virginia or South Carolina. Slavery in this region, although unjust, was tempered by the moral and religious influence of North Carolina's Quakers. It was also influenced by the Methodists, many of whom were abolitionists who shared the common threads of persecution each group had suffered. The cultivation of the land and natural resources gave the region a superior economic advantage. This land of the longleaf pine, known as the Sandhills for its sandy soil, was once North Carolina's leading producer of exports. During the eighteenth and nineteenth centuries, naval stores of extracted turpentine, rosin, pitch, and tar supplied much of Europe and beyond. Yet, as proud as one might be of this accomplishment and of the nickname *The Tar Heel State*, it was not without a price.

During one period in its history," the land of 'pine barrens'" was used to describe the Upper Cape Fear River Valley. This resulted after dense forests of virgin longleaf pines vanished, over several centuries, for lack of a sustainable replanting program. Through the years, there have always been nature conservationists who have strongly expressed their support for more protection of the longleaf pine. Nevertheless, business interests won out due to either the lack of state and federal regulations or weak enforcement. Today, groups such as the Nature Conservancy, the Sandhills Area Land Trust, and Sustainable Sandhills exemplify the ArgyllAmerica spirit by offering a means of coordinated strategy, increasing awareness, and collaborating with groups and communities throughout the region and state.

The ArgyllAmerica I know transcends race, shared by black, white, red, and yellow, and understands and accepts its cultural dynamics. The Argyll Colony in America consists of a unique but determined Scottish people and their descendants. It also references the spirit of those descendants who reside in the "Colony" with the lineage of West Africans and Native Americans who helped shape the region. ArgyllAmerica, while honoring the heritage of its ancestors, seeks to embrace others throughout the world who identify with it. Today, many descendants live outside the region in other parts of the state and country. The origin of ArgyllAmerica is international, with African and European influence, as well as American.

ArgyllAmerica is about the present and, in particular, the future. The establishment of Fort Bragg and Pope Air Field in the 20th century affected the entire region. However, Fayetteville's economy was directly impacted and its growth easily outpaced other contiguous counties and municipalities. Because the United States military was a leader in breaking down the barriers of racial segregation, it helped to define the culture of the region and led to greater racial harmony among its residents, especially through some difficult periods in American history such as the Civil Rights era. Home to the Green Berets and the Special Forces, Fort Bragg is perceived as a resilient place, where men and women prepare to liberate the world's oppressed.

Fast forward to the 21st century, and many will appreciate and embrace the uniqueness of the human spirit, personified through the people, the place, and the principles that originated in this area – even if they are not Scottish, Irish, Scottish-American, Afro-Scottish, African-American, West African, or Native American.

Many of the baby boom generation might remember the Salem cigarette commercial and jingle, before cigarette TV advertising was prohibited: "You can take Salem out of the country, but…you can't take the country out of Salem." Well, ArgyllAmerica is similar. Today, because ArgyllAmerica is a spirit that transcends, it is no longer confined to rural America, though its cultural roots are definitely rural and small town

America. Whether you live in Atlanta, Charleston, Charlotte, Wilmington, Richmond, Los Angeles, New York, or anywhere from sea to shining sea, the Spirit of ArgyllAmerica is there.

The Spirit of ArgyllAmerica seeks to answer two questions, asked through the centuries, as it reveals itself: "Who do you belong to?" "Where do you come from?"

Let us pursue the spirit.

1

Market House

"We shall come up slowly and painfully perhaps, but we shall win our way."

- Charles Waddell Chestnutt

The month of May in the American South is one of the most special times of the year. The weather is moderate to warm, and the multiple colors of spring form a picturesque spectrum, as flowers, trees, and other plants, nurtured by April's rain, now seem more awake and in full bloom. The chirping of birds and the subtle buzzing of insects in the distance create an innate theatrical soundtrack. Hints of summer, with its heat and humidity, are in the air, letting us know that it is around the corner. The sweet smells of wildflowers serve as natural air freshener in the prevailing breezes as they travel through the longleaf pines of the Sandhills.

Back home in metro Atlanta, as everywhere in America, people were being encouraged to complete the U.S. Census, this first year of the second decade of the 21st century.

I periodically came "Home To My Valley," as literary giant Paul Green, also native to the same Upper Cape Fear River Valley, often did. On this visit, I was drawn to downtown Fayetteville, North Carolina. This was not the norm for me. Nevertheless, my curiosity led me there that warm Saturday evening. I had to satisfy a piece of nostalgia, held over, deep within. I would find it on Hay Street. But things had also changed. That evening,

I saw a slow, albeit cosmopolitan street with wide sidewalks of red brick pavers. I could see businesses of yesteryear on the off streets, the fringes. Here, I saw clubs, side-walk cafes, and restaurants with people sharing time and space. Condos overlooked the street, now lined with beautiful oaks, inter-racial couples held hands, black lamp posts wrapped with small white lights glistened with an aura of perhaps a new day – a new era, dawning.

I remembered how I looked forward to going to nearby "Fayettenam" as a youngster, especially Hay Street. Fayetteville, the commercial, corporate, and cultural regional center of the former Argyll Colony, was a refreshing change from my friendly rural village, located twenty minutes north in the adjacent bedroom county, up the former plank road. From my youthful perspective, there seemed to be a lot of activity in downtown Fayetteville, and as this was before the coming of Cross Creek Mall, people actually shopped in the small businesses and department stores that lined the thoroughfare. As in many military towns, prostitutes often walked the popular street at night, looking for lonesome soldiers a long way from home, making my juvenile mind even more curious.

Although some might say that the Hay Street of that era was sleazy, it is an understatement to say that the military presence of nearby Fort Bragg and Pope Air Force Base significantly influenced the culture of this former capital city in the 1960s. America was engaged in an unpopular war in Vietnam and it was a time defined by the Kent State student massacres, civil rights unrest such as the Greensboro sit-ins, experimentation with illicit drugs, and the flower children of the hippie generation.

The extraordinarily talented but troubled multiple Grammy Award winner Marvin Gaye seemed to capture the pulse of America at this time. In his 1971 album of the same name, he asked the country, "What's Going On?" as he crooned:

> "… *Father, Father*
> *We don't need to escalate*
> *You see, war is not the answer*
> *For only love can conquer hate…*
>
> *… I'll tell you*
> *What's going on.*"

Marvin's message still resonates today, some four decades later.

It's hard not to notice the Market House, a beautiful red brick example of "eighteenth-century English town halls with an open arcaded ground floor, a second story containing one or more public rooms, and a hipped roof surmounted by a cupola," as described by the National Register of Historic Places. Built in 1838 to replace the building burned in 1831, the Market House was legally registered on Gillespie Street and located in a circle at the junction of Green, Person, and Hay Streets. Through the years, the Market House, a National Historic Landmark, has had a variety of uses. In the new millennium, it has been used for offices, an art museum, and a library.

Photo: Market House, Fayetteville, NC
Credit: Bennett Scarborough; Scarborough Photography

The Market House I know, at least the picture formed in my mind in its early years, is very vivid, archaic, and busy. Its sights, smells, and sounds conjure up thoughts of what it might have been like several generations after the Argyll Colony formed, back in the days when the region was maturing from being a colony to part of a state. When I digest the events of the past that surround this significant structure, my "mental picture" goes back to a time and place where some people, black and white, still spoke Gaelic, the language of "the stranger."

My youngest brother, Herbert, had accompanied me from Georgia, the *Empire State of the South*. We stood there, patiently waiting on the sidewalk adjacent to the circle, anticipating that the chimes would ring from the cupola as they have done through the ages, the last one of the evening now a historical reference.

While reminiscing, I vaguely remembered hearing the chimes

while shopping with my parents or perhaps even later as a teen, walking the streets or going to the evening movies. Rarely did I really focus on them, for what is a reminder of the time to the young?

Many years later, I discovered through an official Fayetteville website that the cupola rings at 9 p.m. for curfew. Oh, yes, to hear the last chime of the day was why I was there! For the last chime signifies a part of the history of Fayetteville prior to the Emancipation Proclamation. The Market House marks the spot where the Constitution of the United States was adopted. The last chime tells a story before and after the Market House came into being. The last chime is symbolic of curfew time – for all slaves.

As I looked at this centrally located structure, I tried to remember the story of how most of the Scottish Highlanders were eager to get here, many years before the erecting of this famous building. I am also reminded of how many slaves who survived the Middle Passage made the journey inland. They and their descendants often were sold here, up to the time of abolition. They, too, have a story.

Now 2100 hours, military time, I anxiously looked northeasterly toward the Market House. As I stood near the historical marker on the circle, signifying the General Assembly's 1789 charter of the University of North Carolina, I was stunned. There was no chime! Perhaps I was mistaken.

I looked at the Market House's clock, its Roman numerals keeping perfect time. A friendly street vendor - a young, black man with "dread-locks" wearing a white "wife beater" T-shirt started a conversation with me, hoping that I would buy his cologne and other items he displayed on a carrying case.

Five minutes past nine o'clock. Still no chime! My brother and I look perplexed at each other as I began to feel a little disappointment replace my anticipation. Herbert, who had crossed the street a few minutes before 9 p.m., now stood directly underneath the white ceiling of the Market House's ground floor.

On entering the west side of the Market House, I paused, recogniz-ing the name of Charles Waddell Chestnutt and his quote, "*We shall come up slowly and painfully perhaps, but we shall win our way.*" I then repeated the words in my head, absorbing them very gradually – proud that the community would recognize him at such a place.

Chestnutt, an African American author, essayist, and entrepreneur was a pioneer in African American literature. He gained success for his novel *The House Behind the Cedars* and *The Conjure Woman*, a collection of short stories and many other literary pieces. He was born a mulatto in Cleveland, Ohio, in 1858 of two free parents who were Fayetteville natives. He lived in Fayetteville, Spartanburg, Charlotte, and South Carolina from 1866, the year after the Civil War, to shortly after Reconstruction; his frustration with the rise of the white supremacy movement caused him to return to his native Cleveland. While a resident of Fayetteville, Chesnutt, who could often "pass" for white, was educated at the Howard School, constructed by the Freedman's Bureau, and was a pupil teacher, assistant principal, and principal of the State Colored Normal School. Today, this school is home to Fayetteville State University.

Having joined my baby brother, we alertly greeted other night-time tourists. They were taking the opportunity to stop, read, and chat before continuing down the street. I yearned to tell them the story – the truth that I see and that I seek. It is the truth about who we are and where we come from. I spare them as they are total strangers, but as they leave I think of the story they did not hear.

CO AS A THA THU? CO LEIS A THA THU?

From Wilmington, they then journeyed slowly up a river, whose waters mirrored the color of tea, winding through dense and mighty forests of green longleaf pines to a place where the bleached sandy soil, derived from sediments produced by an ancient river delta, covered the undulating earth with abundance.

Even in the stifling humid heat of summer, they were still excited about the uncertainty that lay ahead of them. The sweet smell of "flowering honeysuckle" and "wild jasmine" and "the wild grape climbing the tall trees" stimulated their minds and noses, inciting even more curiosity.

The Royal Governor of North Carolina, Gabriel Johnston, born in Scotland, welcomed fellow Highland Scots from places with names like Colonsay, Gigha, Islay, Jura, and Kintyre with open arms and land grants, and to a country free of religious persecution and high taxes.

Yet on different boats and at different times, others came for different reasons and from different places of origin.

They would arrive against their will to a place called Campbellstown and Cross Creek. Fayetteville, as it would be later known, was the regional market or shopping town. Goods and services were traded at this stop, a city of commerce off the Cape Fear River. However, this stop was also a slave town…

Dě ṅ t-anm a tha ort?
What's your name?

Ciamar a tha thu?
 How are you?

 Tha gu math, tapadh leat.
Fine, thanks!

Co ás a tha sibh?
Where are you from?

Cáit' a bheil thu/sibh á dol?
Where are you going?

These were common exchanges as newly arrived immigrants from Argyll, Scotland, were greeted by family and friends, settlers in a new American colony.

The immigrants nearby were overheard by the enslaved people worn from a treacherous Trans-Atlantic passage, which took them --frightened, chained, and shackled, two by two, in the belly of the feces-laden slave ship, from the shores of West Africa to this strange new land of blackwater rivers, sand hills, and green pine thickets.

Co as a tha thu?
Where do you come from?

Co leis a tha thu?
Who do you belong to?

These people, now enslaved and lacking any comprehension of this "chattering" – a new language being heard, constantly in their ears –could see, based on the settlers' body language, inflection of their voices, and the positive responses received, that these words were terms of endearment. These warm-hearted words were directed to the Scottish immigrants as they got off the buggy at a corner of Hay Street. Over the years, many would eventually learn the language of their slave masters – Gaelic.

I imagine seeing these beautiful black people, now in bondage, in chains, still proud, physically tired, but not spiritually broken from a horrific journey, seem to ask of each other, many not yet acquainted, "Where do you come from? Who do you belong to?" However, I see them speaking but do not understand them – yet. Could they be the tribal languages, such as Ebu, Igbo, Mande, Wolof, Bantu, Hausa, Yoruba, etc.? I also picture some enslaved persons on the block looking around this very diverse group, linked together not only by metal but a shared experience, frustrated at not being able to understand the tribal language of others, but excited and relieved when discovering someone who did.

This three-dimensional imagery isn't fair as I see the enslaved parting, some belonging to the same family, split up, crying and pleading to be free...to be together. Separated from their family and friends in Fayetteville, they would now reside on farms throughout the region called Clark, Murchison, McPherson, Gilchrist, Swann, Blue, Buie, Harrington, McNeill, Shaw and those of a lot of other Argyll Colony families. Simultaneously, I see Scottish clans join, singing, dancing and being merry, also in the Cape Fear River Valley to seek a newfound freedom.

Governor Johnston never saw the Market House but it is a fact that he issued many land grants, especially to Scots, and was very welcoming. Nevertheless, many years later, slaves were sold at Fayetteville's Market House, up to time of abolition.

That is not my imagination!

However, my point is not to discuss the cruelty or the merits of slavery, or whether Highland Scots had an inside track or advantage when they entered the Argyll Colony. Slavery was brutal and immoral! Yet, some enslaved persons in certain regions or performing certain jobs were treated better than others! History tells us that the Scots suffered mightily in their native land, especially after falling to the British at the Battle of Culloden. This defeat instilled a certain level of humility and empathy for others, especially the persecuted and downtrodden. No, my position is just the opposite! Somehow, the same God that Paul prayed to and received divine inspiration from to write Ephesians and other biblical books allowed for my ancestors, against their free will, to leave the palm coasts and tropical climate of Africa. In America, they would meet the Highland Scots, initially not as partners, but after institutional bondage, trials, and tribulations, they would later become friends and neighbors, dwelling in the valley of the longleaf pine.

Whether Market House or the "big house," this was for many the beginning of the fusion of cultures.

I did not hear the 9 p.m. bell chiming from the cupola tonight. Thank God we live in a day when it chimes no longer for me --- for I am, on the backs of my ancestors, the resilient, and those who pursued racial harmony, free.

2

Cameron Hill

A pur'olo oche (Still in the land of the living)
- Indigenous Bubi expression

I was a young adult when my father first told me that buried in the "black section" of the white-owned Cameron Hill Presbyterian Church Cemetery was his father, Royal Gilchrist, and paternal grandfather, Abraham Gilchrist. I was stunned.

"Black section? Mmn," I pondered.

Up until that time, I did not know that blacks were buried there, at all! Flora MacDonald, a Scottish heroine, lived on the "Hill" while attending Barbeque Presbyterian Church when she resided in the area in the 18th century. While growing up as a kid, I frequently read the historical marker about Mrs. MacDonald by the roadside when passing by on NC Highway 24 in the Sandhills. I recognized that she was very important early on, but never associated Cameron Hill as being the place where two very close relatives and perhaps numerous others were buried. These respective burials were many years before integration in the South. Even though they were not quite integrated with the white cemetery, they were still in close proximity. You see, Daddy's father died when Daddy was less than one year old, and my paternal great-grandfather, Abraham, died in 1918. It would be another nine years before Leonard, my father, was born. It seemed he never had much of an emotional attachment to his parents' ancestry. At least, it did not show outwardly.

Many decades later, I would become closer to actualizing my cultural identity. It was a grey overcast morning sky on Martin Luther King Day. I was visiting Mom and Dad, buried nearby on a hill with a beautiful view, in Johnsonville A.M.E. Zion Church Cemetery, off NC Highway 27. As I turned right off Sabastian Lane, driving down the dirt cemetery road, I became anxious as I looked to the left, passing several equally spaced white posts, wondering whether I remembered which side Mom and Dad were buried on, in relation to each other.

"Whew!" I said to myself, as I stepped out of my grey Ford Freestyle and into the loose, sandy soil. "I was right," I affirmed quietly, with a sigh of relief. I continued talking to myself, under my breath, "Mom on the left and Dad on the right." It was as if I were a child again, wanting to keep it a secret that I had to think about their placement. As usual, when visiting my parents, whose memories are still fresh in my mind, I prayed, interspersed with my conversation with them.

THANK YOU, LORD, FOR THIS DAY, AND THE OPPOR-TUNITY TO VISIT MY PARENTS. THANK YOU, GOD, FOR BLESSING ME WITH TWO OUTSTANDING PARENTS, WHO INSTILLED IN ME THE VALUES OF RESPECT FOR ELDERS, FOR OTHERS, AND FOR HARD WORK. Mom and Dad, today is Martin Luther King, Jr.'s birthday celebration – but you probably already know that, don't you. I imagine you both are up there in Heaven with Martin rejoicing with him and others who have crossed over. This is a glorious time on Earth with today being MLK day, one day before Barack Hussein Obama's inauguration and his being sworn in as our nation's 44th President, its first African-American. Oh! I wish you were here in the flesh so that you could share this moment in time and history, but you probably already know. THANK YOU, LORD, FOR MOM AND DAD, FOR IF THERE WERE NO ERMA AND LEONARD, THERE WOULD BE NO ERNEST ROYAL GILCHRIST. AMEN!

Ernest R. Gilchrist

I looked to Heaven, holding back tears, and smiled, with a warm but heavy heart, for this was a time of rejoicing. I then looked downward to the Earth's soil, swallowing my saliva, and as I always did, read the scriptural verse engraved on the tombstones of each parent, from left to right.

Erma Clark Gilchrist
ABIDETH FAITH HOPE CHARITY THESE
THREE BUT THE GREATEST OF THESE IS LOVE

Leonard Wesley Gilchrist
I WAITED PATIENTLY FOR THE LORD AND HE
INCLINED UNTO ME AND HEARD MY CRY

After reading the tombstones, I walked to the opposite or westside of the granite stones, over the closely cut brown wiregrass, inspecting their graves, which still had residual from the small mounds of dirt on them, shaped by the mortician's burial crew. As I looked to the east and stood between their tombstones, I saw, over in the distance, the ridgeline that Buffalo Lake Road rides. This view of natural beauty always conjured up images of what experts believed to have been an ancient Buffalo grazing trail that the Indians once traveled.

Dad once said after Mom's passing that she had selected her final resting place in the cemetery, located at its highest vantage point.

I left the church cemetery, still with a trace of mourning, heading southwest on NC Highway 27, observing the now mature subdivisions on either side of the road. I soon arrived at the intersection of Highway 24. I looked right in the direction of the sleepy, but once thriving little town of Cameron.

Still in my reflective mood, a thought occurred to me in what seemed to be a split second, causing my heart to ache. It was one of those awkward thoughts, too. It was the massacre by the Cape Fear Indians and an event known as The Day the Birds Kept Singing. The thought of the Cape Fear Indians massacring almost all of the Drowning Creek Indians, many years ago, just a few miles to my west towards Cameron, seemed sad. This tragic event really happened. It happened simply because the Drowning Creek Indians crossed over into the Cape Fear hunting territory – looking for food, which had become scarce in their area.

A minute later, I drove up the incline, slowly onto the yard of the small modest red-brick Cameron Hill Church, with great expectations, but still a particular amount of uncertainty.

Historic Cameron Hill Presbyterian Church,
Johnsonville Township, NC

As my vehicle came to a stop, I remembered what I had previously read once, concerning the Cameron Hill Church of the Cape Fear settlement as described by 20st century resident historian Ed Cameron:

"Cameron Hill stands tall, a place of interest to all who pause to contemplate the imprints of time that has passed. The essence of its history is not to be found in the rendering of facts... In early days it was a wee bit Scotland removed. A people, often honor-bound to favor a king that was hated. A people by nature clannish and nostalgic, thus bound to a homeland that had become too harsh to endure, when there was hope in America. Only the brave would come, seeking relief, land, and independence."

Towering over the pines from across the road was the Cameron Hill Fire Tower, with its own sense of history and purpose – the original one being the first lookout tower in North Carolina on private land.

Keeping watch over those who came this way was Flora MacDonald's historical marker, planted several hundred feet away. This would be my first trip actually walking the hallowed ground where some of my closest ancestors lie, near the deceased descendants of Scottish Highlanders, up on the Hill. Much of my lifetime had passed me by before making this journey.

Scottish Heroine Flora MacDonald's Historical Marker at Cameron Hill Presbyterian Church, NC

Yet, in my heart, with reverence, the connection had already been made the day Dad first told me that they lay buried there. Nevertheless, I almost felt ashamed, letting previous opportunities go unfulfilled to pay my respects.

As I got out of the car and walked down the sloping paved road, assuming the "black cemetery" would be at the rear of the property, I then realized how impractical my goal was. I needed help. I reached for my cell phone and called Brian, my childhood friend and schoolmate, who just happened to be white and of Scottish Highlander ancestry. I told him that I missed seeing him at Campbell on the Saturday that just passed, for the Jacksonville University Men's basketball game, but understood. Brian shared with me that his wife Donna was not feeling well that day and that he felt it necessary to stay close. They both attended Cameron Hill, and Donna's family was from a long line of Camerons that founded this historic church.

Then I said, suddenly, "I'm at Cameron Hill Church, trying to find my ancestors' graves. Where are my ancestors buried?"

Brian said, "Look for a clearing beyond the church cemetery's graves and you will see some big oak trees. It's probably the most beautiful area of the cemetery."

With the phone to my left ear and facing east, I turned to my right, looked up the "Hill," and saw two huge beautiful Turkey Oaks. There was a third, ghostly, oak tree nearby that I could tell had witnessed a lot of history. It appeared to be dead, its core rotten.

"Wow! Thanks, Brian!"

One tall, gangly but strong oak tree stood out more than the rest. This tree, with its chiseled arms, sprouting everywhere, was larger than the others. It leaned to the east, as if to suggest a longing for the Cape Fear River, Mother Africa, or the Highlands of southwestern Scotland, known as the "Coast of Gaels."

Based on the diameter and width of this tree which had me fascinated, it appeared to be more than 150 to 200 years old. As I stood there, gawking upwards at this feat of nature, I imagined it bearing witness to the Scottish Gaelic-speaking preachers who ministered to the parishioners in the 18th and 19th centuries, and to my enslaved ancestors, conversing in the same tongue. Could it have witnessed great-grandpa Abraham's birth in 1838, Reverend Jackson "Uncle Jack" Murchison, a supercentenarian, growing local churches, and General Sherman's army on their way to Fayetteville?

*Photo: Sprawling Oak Tree at Cameron Hill
Presbyterian Church Cemetery*

This tree was there, I am sure, when Frederick Law Olmsted passed through the Sandhills in 1856, only two years later to be awarded the job to create New York City's Central Park.

This sprawling tree might have witnessed former slaves passing by, passionately rejoicing because of President Lincoln's Emancipation Proclamation, hearing them repeat what others sang joyously from Boston's Tremont Temple, "Sound the land timbrel o'er Egypt's dark sea, Jehovah hath triumphed, his people are free."

This shapely tree was a curious onlooker when northern carpetbaggers roamed the "sand barrens" during Reconstruction.

In November 1939, this tree must have listened! Surely it heard the Carolina Playmakers perform Paul Green's *The Highland Call* in Fayetteville's LaFayette Opera House, amongst closed schools and the community's nervousness about an outbreak of polio.

Yes, if only this tree could talk, it would tell me how it witnessed the nourishing of naval stores and timber products in the "pine barrens," the emergence of tobacco, replacing cotton as the cash crop, and the Scotsman Donald Ross, on his way to Overhills and the Rockefeller Estate to design a signature golf course.

I say, if this mammoth tree could talk, it would tell us how it survived through the years, soaking up water and nutrients from underground springs, mostly tributaries, which still come from what was once named the Rio Jordan by Spaniards, centuries ago, later to be known as the Cape Fear River.

This tree has a lot to say, for it was not far through the woods, to the southeast, where the U.S. Government built Fort Bragg in 1918. This mighty oak listened when, in 1961, President John F. Kennedy visited the military base and authorized that the green beret be used exclusively by the U.S. Special Forces – *De Oppresso Liber* ("To Liberate the Oppressed").

This tree is bursting with knowledge about the birth of Pinehurst in 1895, great men such as James Walker Tufts and sons, Frazier Gilchrist's birth in 1875, grandpa Royal's sudden passing in 1927, joint annual Easter Sunrise service at area churches, both black and white, and the numerous people buried at Cameron Hill, with marked and unmarked tombstones.

Most of all, if this big towering oak could talk, it would express its appreciation to Brian and several leaders, black and white, who led the efforts of the community coming together to clean up and restore the cemetery's "black section," a meaningful resting place on a famous hill in what was once known as the Argyll Colony.

I began to walk the cemetery's "black section," hoping that, somehow, I would miraculously find my ancestors' graves marked. Dad had already told me that they were not marked. Somewhat discouraged, I began to walk the old adjacent white section of the cemetery, trying to determine the connection, if any, that binds the countless Scots – Camerons, Hickmans, Mangums, Johnsons, Browns, McLeans, etc. – with me and my relatives. Condensation from the tree's leaves above my head began to drip on my black leather cap, causing me to remove it and shake it slightly.

"Who am I?" I asked myself emphatically. "Why am I here?" I asked rhetorically, and sensed a little frustration within my spirit. "What is the connection between my roots and this cemetery?" I wondered silently.

Returning to the big oak, I picked up four acorns. "Four," I said prophetically. "I am the fourth generation from Abraham, a founder of

Johnsonville A.M.E. Zion Church, shortly after the Civil War," I said to myself, assuredly.

These golden-colored acorns were everywhere under the shouldering arms of the huge tree, some hiding underneath the beautiful wide, brown leaves, leftover from yet another fall foliage season. These acorns, two with crowns, and two without, were a pleasant flashback to a distant childhood memory, and they reminded me that this eastward leaning tree was still alive and bearing fruit.

FROM SILK-COTTON TREE TO OAK TREE

As I stood underneath the mighty sprawl of the centuries old oak tree's embrace, I realized that many of the unanswered questions in my life were in this cemetery. Perhaps, that may sound morbid to some, but as I began to look around Cameron Hill, my assignment was clear. Just as I surmise that my ancestors once asked these questions, in their adopted Scottish Gaelic tongue, "*Co as a tha thu? Co leis a tha thu? (Where do you come from? Who do you belong to?)*, I must find the answers to those simple questions, but in their native tongue.

Many historians tell us that culture and identity are closely associated to any language. In ArgyllAmerica, this provides major insights into why many blacks and whites have, although not perfect, close social, cultural and religious relationships. In 1872, the Reverend J.C. Sinclair wrote the following about the use of Gaelic in the Upper Cape Fear Valley:

> "*The old race is gone and their descendants have given up, in a great degree, the customs and manners of the old Gaels... There is no Gaelic preached in the Carolinas now and not likely to be any in the future... I have met with a number of coloured people who speak the Gaelic as well as if they had been raised in any of the Hebrides.*"

In the Carolinas, many African-Americans had become as fluent as "White" people in speaking Gaelic and had mastered Highland music, especially on the banjo. I'm not sure why Gaelic seemed to have lasted longer in "black" churches in the Cape Fear Valley than in "white" churches. During the Reconstruction of American history, which was roughly the decade that followed the Civil War, although Gaelic was dying out, many African-Americans were as fluent in Gaelic as the native Scots.

Several months prior to my visit to Cameron Hill, I happened upon a genealogical fair in Decatur, Georgia, at the Dr. William C. Brown Public Library, sponsored by the Afro-American Historical and Genealogical Society, Inc. – Metro Atlanta Chapter. My daughter was visiting the Decatur branch of the DeKalb County Library System, located on Wesley Chapel Road, and I needed to kill some time while I waited.

On my way into the building, I saw two tall men who were Buffalo Soldier enactors, there to participate in the fair's activities. They were chatting with some vendors who were deep frying fish. The aroma was irresistible. One of the men, whom I had met earlier in the year for the first time, was my distant cousin on my father's side, and he informed me that some interesting activities were going on in the library's community room. The other tall, lanky enactor just happened to be an associate and fellow government employee named RJ. He informed me that if I wanted to buy some fish, I had to go into the library to buy a ticket and then return to the vendors. After some brief conversation, I said thanks and continued walking down the sidewalk towards the red brick library.

My timing seemed perfect, for I had wanted to learn more about my ancestry before circa 1800. Like most blacks in the Americas, knowing exactly where my African ancestry originated from represents the missing link. I entered the library's community room as someone was speaking about genealogy. Moments later they prepared to do a raffle for winning a premium ancestry test kit (using one's DNA), offered by African Ancestry, Inc.

"Get a chance to discover your African ancestry for only seven dollars," the meeting leader said.

I reached for my wallet, opened it, found $12…and paused. I knew that the fish sandwich was five dollars, and I really wanted to get some of that hot, mouth-watering fish. The calculation I was doing in my head was simple. Mmn! If I took a chance on the raffle, I'd be broke.

"Okay," I thought. "Take a $7 chance on the raffle versus paying $300 to buy one kit, if I do not win." The drawing was almost ready to begin when I sprang up from my chair and walked to the rear of the room to get a ticket. "Here goes," I said. Well! Did I say it was a raffle? I was soon to be broke because my taste buds were still set on eating some hot, mouth-watering fish, afterwards. However, I did get a brochure for an African Ancestry DNA kit before leaving the meeting room.

Two days later, while at the Subway® on East Ponce de Leon Avenue in downtown Decatur, lunching on a turkey sandwich, I called African Ancestry, located in a Washington, DC, suburb, and inquired about doing the DNA testing to determine my family's ancestry. Up to this point, this act was the closest I had ever come to making the big step. I had known about testing from watching *African American Lives*, a documentary written and produced by Dr. Henry Louis "Skip" Gates, Jr., a Harvard University professor and scholar. Before then, I had become intrigued by an article in the *Atlanta Journal-Constitution*, featuring former United Nations Ambassador and City of Atlanta Mayor Andrew Young, and how he had participated in the testing, tracing his roots back to the Mende people of Sierra Leone. Kelli, a friendly employee of African Ancestry, really impressed me with her competency and warm cordial spirit. Although I had received a brochure from my visit to the library a month earlier and had already checked out their website, I asked her to explain the PatriClan™ test and the MatriClan™.

Kelli very patiently explained that "the PatriClan™ Test traces paternal ancestry by analyzing the Y chromosome that males inherit exclusively from their fathers."

"Tell me about the other test, the MatriClan™ Test," I requested, with much curiosity.

"The MatriClan™ Test traces maternal ancestry by analyzing mito-chondrial DNA, which men and women inherit exclusively from their mothers," Kelli answered.

A few weeks later, after my visit to Cameron Hill, I anxiously ordered both test kits.

After much anticipation, the package containing the test kits from African Ancestry finally arrived. Synetha, my wife, sitting at one end of the kitchen table, urged me to open it.

I picked it up off the speckled brown marble counter top, walked toward her with excitement, and with two hands holding the small white cardboard box above my head, skyward, turned to the east, and said, "Is you the one?"

Synetha thought I was stupid and shook her head, silently. We both then laughed outwardly, but inwardly I was dead serious. What might have appeared to be a comical reenactment of a scene from *The Lion King*, depicting the celebration of a new life that could possibly lead his or her people, actually was a question to God.

"WILL THE RESULTS OF THESE DNA TESTS, BOTH MATERNAL AND PATERNAL, EMPOWER MY FAMILY AND COMMUNITY AND LEAD US TO A NEW LEVEL OF CULTURAL AND ETHNIC IDENTITY?"

Nearly six weeks had passed since sending off the kits to Silver Spring, Maryland. At last, that long awaited day arrived. Synetha was minutes away from meeting me at Publix on GA Highways 212 & 138 in Conyers to make a transfer with my daughter Tamara and our neighbor's kid, "Tre", who both had a 4 p.m. appointment with the same math tutor. It had been raining heavily that day. In fact, I noticed that the amount of rainfall overnight had begun to flood the low lying areas near the South River, located near the house on Oglesby Bridge Road. Synetha pulled up right beside me to my left, as I waited patiently in the grocery store parking lot near the road.

As the kids got out of the Freestyle and into our 11-year old Infiniti *i*30, she raised a white package that apparently had been lying on her passenger seat, smiled, and said, "It's here."

"Knowing you, I'm surprised you haven't opened it already," I said, jokingly.

"No. I thought you should be the one to open it first," she replied. "Then you can share the results with me," she added.

I nodded my head in agreement, as if to say that she had made a wise decision. We kissed each other from our respective cars with "smooches" and drove off in different directions.

Finally arriving in Lithonia, we entered Monica's house. Monica, a close family friend and my wife's physical therapy colleague, would periodically allow the kids to use her dining room as a study area when Elijah, a high school math teacher, needed an alternative to the library to tutor them.

With the DNA test results in hand, I walked nervously into Monica's den and sat down. I could not have envisioned a more appropriate environment, with its numerous pieces of West African artwork – tribal masks, carvings, paintings, murals, etc. – to be the place where I would realize my MatriClan® and PatriClan® identity. Anxious, I added unintentionally to my anxiety by getting up to walk around the room, soaking up my visual heritage. Monica had collected quite a few pieces of black art.

"I am impressed," I said inwardly, and returned to the couch. I paused and prayed silently, before beginning to open the package. "Bum-Bum, Bum-Bum, Bum-Bum-Bum-Bum-Bum-Bum, Bum-Bum…"; I could feel the drumbeats of West Africa moving rapidly in my chest, as my heart raced with incredible velocity, sensing a signature life experience was about to take place. With the package finally opened, there seemed to be incredible silence, as if the drumbeats stopped, while I held my breath. I opened the beautiful brown floral print folder from African Ancestry.

"The mitochondrial DNA (mtDNA) sequence that we determined from your sample share ancestry with the Tikar people of Cameroon today," revealed the letter from Gina Page, President. I breathed in, not just by necessity but also with relief and excitement.

"Mmn! Cameroon, huh." I said in a pleasantly stunned and very satisfied manner.

"We are halfway there!" I said, with a sense of accomplishment, knowing that these results were not just limited to me.

"The Y chromosome DNA markers that we determined from your samples share ancestry with the Bubi people in Bioko Island (Equatorial Guinea) today," the letter from African Ancestry confirmed.

"Now that's interesting," I said, wondering exactly where Equatorial Guinea and Bioko Island were located. I called my wife so that she could be the first to know.

"Are you pleased, now that you know?" she asked.

"I am on cloud nine. Can't you tell?" I replied excitedly.

Next, I eagerly called several siblings, even my sister Joyce who, along with her husband Keith and youngest daughter, was military and stationed in South Korea. It was 6:30 a.m. Sunday morning there, and I could tell I awakened her. They received the news with much interest and humility.

Minutes later, I called Yàw, that is, Dr. Bismarck Appiah-Kubi, and shared my new-found identity. Bismarck is a former general practitioner, a genetics specialist, and one of my best friends. However, I felt it necessary to pay him a visit, as well. A few hours later, I drove to Norcross, another Atlanta suburb, to see him. Appiah-Kubi is an Ashanti, whose native roots are in the Kumasi region of Ghana. When he was at an early age, his "Uncle Willie, a Ghanaian roving ambassador, took him to London to live with him. Educated in the best private schools, he later went to medical school in Scotland, finishing at the top of his class. The beautiful thing about my brother Bismarck is that he is a patient teacher, educating me about the world beyond Atlanta and America with a balanced perspective.

Bismarck reviewed the package and, being a trained physician, began to analyze the results before him. He read, "99.7% sequence similarity for the mitochondrial DNA," as if I did not know.

"Through our mother's lineage, my siblings and I are almost 100% African, going all the way back to Cameroon!" I proudly shouted.

"But not 100% - you need three tenths of one percent," he said, jokingly.

He continued on, reviewing the document.

"Impressive!" Bismarck said, with a more serious, studious expression.

"Yes! My Y chromosome is traceable 100% back to Bioko Island," I said, as I stood up and walked in Bismarck's direction. "I'm as African as you!" I said, sticking my chest out, proudly.

I looked down at my beloved, intelligent, and very cultured friend and quoted a lyric from Peter Tosh, a key member of the Wailers, which I first became aware of through him: "no matter where you come from, so long as you're a black man you are an African." Biz', as I often called him, loved Reggae music and introduced me to the greater awareness of this deceased 6'-5 ½" Jamaican musician many years ago.

He began to bob his head and said, in his very articulate American English, "Peter Tosh, the màn!"

I now sense a greater connection to why I was at Cameron Hill that drizzly overcast day, paying homage to some of my paternal ancestors as they lay buried in unmarked graves, near the wingspan of the magnificent gangly oak tree. No, I have never been to Equatorial Guinea's Bioko Island, the "Amazon of Africa," home of my paternal Y chromosome ancestors, but it is indescribable the kinship I feel at this moment. Fernando Po, as it was once known for hundreds of years until 1979, and named for its discoverer,

Fernão Pŏ, is a tropical paradise and once described by British explorer Sir Harry H. Johnston as one of the most beautiful islands on earth.

The indigenous people of Bioko, the Bubi (Boobe) refer to their lush island in many ways, according to their diverse geographical district and tribe: "*Oche* (N), *Otcho* (E), *Oiso* (NE), *Oricho* (S), *Oncho and Aboncho* (SW)." This island, approximately 20 miles off the coast of Cameroon, rises sharply from the sea, evidence that it was once part of the mainland until approximately 14,000 years ago, when the Ice Age ended and the waters rose.

According to Philip Curtin, noted Johns Hopkins University professor, author, and historian, during the period of 1700 to 1807, 40% of enslaved West Africans that left from the Bight of Biafra were in British ships. I am deducing that, on this extinct volcanic island, my ancestors may have been taken from Moka (Riabbi), where a large concentration of Bubi people live today. This educated guess is based on the findings of a German ethnographer who, in 1916, spoke to Bubi informants.

These indigenous people told him "whites never penetrated much farther inland than about Moka because the Bubi, in spite of being armed with only spears, were too dangerous for them, the Bubi knew the terrain and [because] the whites would be easily overpowered in the thick vegetation."

I can't imagine what must have been a chilling moment when, for the last time, the captives, including my ancestor, knew there was no return to Fernando Po (Bioko) – never again to see the 9,480 foot Mount Santa Isabel, towering over the north side of the large island. Never again would he be able to admire the natural beauty of its mangrove swamps and its lush tropical rainforests. So emotional this parting must have been for a people who, historically, fled the mainland hundreds of years prior to seek liberty, only to find themselves in captivity.

I envision the real possibility of a poor mother, deep in the forests, who has cried a monsoon of tears since discovering that her husband has been captured, say, "*Obaue, boobem; oipodi boobem* ('*Good-bye, my spouse*')."

Likewise, many miles away, is one of many captives – her husband and father to her children – in the dark, putrid-smelling bowel of a slave ship. I imagine seeing him as he somberly watches children being brought down below, frightened, crying and trembling, more males than females.

As the vessel would have left the harbor in Malabo, now the capital city of Equatorial Guinea and largest city on Bioko Island, he might have mouthed silently to himself, with a broken heart – "*Obaue, boarim; oipodi boarim ('Good-bye, my spouse')*" and "*Obaue, Oche ('Good-bye, Fernando Po')*."

My mind is overwhelmed with the thought of what my ancestor's Equatoguinean culture was like in the 18th century when he undoubtedly came to the Americas. I do know that those coming from the Bight of Biafra were "a major player in the development of the African-based community in North America."

Fitting, isn't it, that the lineage of my father's father and my father's father's father, too, came from the land of the silk-cotton tree to rest under this huge oak tree. The silk-cotton tree or ceiba tree, in Spanish, Equatorial Guinea's official language, is also referred to as the God tree.

I have found my connection to part of who I am at Cameron Hill. It is an unspectacular but important place that has unknowingly bridged the Spirit of ArgyllAmerica, its past and present, fusing Africa with Europe and America.

Now I know the answers to the questions that many of my ancestors must have asked each other, long after the tribal scars were no longer visible and the lilt of their Bantu language was replaced by Scottish Gaelic and, ultimately, English. For them who died not knowing, I say that I am "*a pur'olo oche*" (*Still in the land of the living*).

I have not forgotten my proud ancestors from the Bantu speaking Tikar people of Cameroon, adjacent to the Bight of Biafra. They will appear again in my story.

3

Paul Green

"Write about the folk you know, and even better, write about the folk you are"
–Professor Frederick Henry Koch

ArgyllAmerica is partly about the pursuit of racial harmony and those who have been or still remain influenced by nature: the ancient beach sands of the Sandhills, the longleaf pine, and the tea-colored water of the Upper Cape Fear River Valley. Paul Green, the author, humanitarian, playwright, poet, and professor, is symbolic of this cultural identity and demonstrated a robust interest in black folk life and elevating race relations. Green, who, in 1927, won a Pulitzer Prize for his stage play In Abraham's Bosom, captured the rudimental essence of rural black life during his time. Although Green would write many plays, three of his more renowned works include Hymn to the Rising Sun, The House of Connelly, and Johnny Johnson. Perhaps Green's most famous and longest running play, The Lost Colony, an outdoor symphonic drama, is still performed today in the Outer Banks of North Carolina. However, this play's theme is historical in context. Green also wrote films for Bette Davis, Clark Gable, and Will Rogers, during his stay in California.

I admire Paul Green because his pursuit of improved race relations, civil rights, and increased empathy for the plight of blacks and the down-trodden required a lot of courage, especially during his era in the segregated South. Many of Green's writings reflected his upbringing in Harnett County, North Carolina, ground zero, along with Cumberland County, as the epicenter of what once was the Argyll Colony. Green called this imaginative re-created rural setting Little Bethel Country, with its own map and landmarks. Similarly, fellow American author and Southerner William Faulkner had his Yoknapatawpha (YOK-na-pa-TAW-pha), set in former Chickasaw Indian territory, in Mississippi. British author Thomas Hardy had his Wessex, set in the south and southwest of England.

Photo: Paul Green - Playwright, author, poet and humanitarian
Credit: Courtesy of Campbell University Archives

Green, a left-handed ambidextrous six-footer with long arms, aspired from his youth to adulthood to reach self-actualization through his love for music, reading, and sports. At ease with blacks, as well as members of his own race, Green grew up working hard in the cotton and tobacco fields of eastern North Carolina. Known in some circles as the "cotton picker," a title he assigned himself early in life because of winning a Harnett County cotton-picking contest, it became a part of his identity for much of his adult life. He witnessed first-hand the work ethic of blacks and other working poor that he labored with and gained their mutual respect.

In December 1922, while attending Cornell University in Ithaca, New York, Green wrote to his father-in-law, Dr. George W. Lay. He openly addressed Dr. Lay, saying that:

> *"…I grew up, as you already know, on the farm among Negroes and tenants. There is no sort of work I haven't done and can't do. I've ditched, rolled logs at a saw-mill, ploughed, hoed, dug stumps, everything. Whatever work was to be done, I must be the champion. I could pull more fodder than any man in the neighborhood. This I demonstrated by beating the title claimer. I could pick more cotton than the other fellow. And this I proved by picking 403 lbs. in ten hours, a record then…"*

Paul Green, a descendant of Scottish immigrants through his dad's lineage, and I walked the same paths but generations apart. He attended Buies Creek Academy, graduating in 1914. In 1926, the Academy became Campbell Junior College, which would eventually become Campbell College and is now Campbell University. I graduated from the University many decades after Green matriculated to attend the University of North Carolina at Chapel Hill. I can appreciate how he must have garnered his love for nature and the agrarian lifestyle. Green's childhood family home in Harnett's Neill's Creek Township is little more than half an hour northeast across the County from my humble childhood home in once very rural Johnsonville Township. The same hard work ethic that Green developed would soon influence me. Like Green, many years later, I toiled in many tobacco fields and family farms on the other side of the Cape Fear River in this same region.

Paul developed a very solid base, having grown up attending numerous churches, along with his mother, Bettie Lorine Byrd Green, in Harnett County. His maternal grandfather was even a minister.

There must have been many students who left Buies Creek Academy to attend Wake Forest College, now Wake Forest University in Winston-Salem, who became fine preachers – ministers and teachers of the Gospel. I'm glad that Paul Green was not one of them.

Attorney William "Bill" A. Johnson, Green's nephew, had lived to be 90 years-old as of 2010. Green genuinely loved "Billy," his sister Mary's son. This was visibly reflected in Paul Green's correspondence directly to the young Johnson, some twenty-six years his junior, and based on comments made about him in letters to Green's sister. The following letter is but one example.

"Dear Billy –

I was surprised to get your letter typewritten. That's a new accomplishment I didn't suspect you of…

Are you going to the University or to Duke when you finish at Buie's Creek, or have you decided to be a peddler or what – maybe a doctor?

Be a smart boy as I know you always will and give my love to Mother, Daddy and the children.

Uncle Paul"

(July 21, 1934)

Photo: Atty William "Bill" Johnson, nephew of Paul Green, and
Ernest Gilchrist outside Green's birth home, relocated to Lillington, NC
Credit: John Wilbourne

According to the wiry former Chair of the UNC Board of Governors, his maternal uncle, in hindsight, "would have had less an impact in the world" had he not gone to the University of North Carolina- Chapel Hill. Paul's father, William Archibald Green, did not like it very much when he realized his son's plan to turn down a full scholarship to Wake Forest College, then based in adjacent Wake County. His father had talked with Reverend James Archibald Campbell, founder of our school, and they had arranged for him to attend the Baptist institution, after graduating from the Academy.

Dr. Campbell told Paul, "Wake Forest is the school for you."

Nevertheless, Paul was determined to go elsewhere and study under teachers like professor of philosophy Horace Williams, saying, "But I want to go to the University (at Chapel Hill), Professor Campbell…"

Reverend Campbell tried to convince him to become a preacher, exclaiming, "Listen, son, if you go there, you're likely to lose your religion… he'll cause you to lose your soul…"

Paul was more influenced by Buies Creek Academy's eccentric redhead, Hubbard Fulton Page, a Harvard-educated English literature professor. In an interview a year before he passed, Green admits to being heavily influenced in his career by Page because of his enthusiasm for his teaching style and his love for literature. These factors created a new level of respect for the "shaggy, tawny head" professor and a personal excitement for the literary realm. Green's writings would later reflect some of the same themes found in Page's 1932 book *Lyrics and Legends of the Cape Fear Country*. This book described the life of people, black and white, in the Upper Cape Fear Valley region, through lyrics and verse.

Paul had a practical faith – a religious man, he displayed both racial harmony and spirituality, all in one, through the actions and words of many of his real-life characters in his stories and plays. The stories of two such characters are shared in the real-life short story of Rassie McLeod and himself, as told in "Rassie and the Barlow Knife," found in Green's *Home To My Valley*. Rassie, a young black boy about Paul's age and the son of a tenant farmer who worked for Paul's dad, did not know color. Neither did Paul.

This story takes place near the close of the 19th century, just over three decades past the end of the Civil War. Green's native Harnett County is the setting for this story, and the impact the war left still casts a shadow over the region. Close friendships were not uncommon between young black and white boys and girls who were playmates in the rural American South, during this era. Through this story, Green shows a depth of feeling and empathy as the very intelligent Rassie and inquisitive Paul interact. Rassie, Green affectionately said, had a lilting voice likened to "the rhythmic phrases of the old-time preachers he quotes so well" and taught him lifelong lessons. The story and the boys' relationship are depicted from Paul's eyes – and heart.

Examples of Green's "color-blindness" and pursuit of racial harmony are rooted in his childhood and revealed in the following excerpts from this classic example of *philia* and *agape* love. In this first passage, Paul's thoughts and words describe the brotherly love, loyalty, and friendship felt for his friend. Here, he describes the time when his dear friend Rassie nicked his finger and bled, while trimming a piece of dogwood, and the dispassionate virtuous love felt after a startling discovery.

"Look-a-there at that!" I said.

"Look-a-there at what?" said Rassie unconcernedly as he wrapped a green oak leaf around his finger and went on scraping and notching the staff.

"At-at your blood-you bleed like that," I said.

"Lawd, just a scratch," said Rassie. "It didn't hurt none, and I aint no whiny-baby. It's bleed to bleed some."

"I mean its red-red same like me when I have the nose-bleed."

Rassie stared at me a moment I can still see him wrinkling his nose.

"Co'sen it's red," he said. And then he spoke up a little sharply, "You figure it'd be differenter?"

"I 'spected maybe-I don't know," I answered, a little shamefaced now before my partner's searching look.

Rassie let out his little dog-yelping laugh. "Mebbe 'cause I'm black you was thinking my blood would be black. Go'way from here, boy! Where you got your brains-in your setter.

And I said I was glad his blood was the same color as mine. And

after that I felt closer to my friend than ever.
And the days were swift and golden then, and I loved my little
black playmate better than father or mother or anybody else in
the whole wide world and I planned that we would stay together
always (Green, Home to My Valley).

One of the most tragic moments in Paul's childhood was when his beloved Rassie died from typhoid fever. Perhaps, Green's most stirring revelation of his brotherhood and love for his friend was also the most sympathetic. Green allows us to feel some of his innermost emotions and thoughts about his practical faith, his love of Christ, as he and his father bury Rassie along the hedgerow at the upper end of a cotton field by a cedar tree. Some might perceive Paul's father as a fair man, but he was also a product of the times. In many ways, Paul had a maturity and a vision that his dad, and even his half-sister Alda, did not have. In this part of the story, at Rassie's burial, Paul, thinking that his father's prayer was not in depth enough, creates, identifies, and plants a stake in the ground.

"It was evening now and almost dark, but I got an old shovel from
the little crib, and we went up into the fields and there under the
big cedar tree we dug Rassie's grave and buried him. And when we
were ready to go, I said, "Ain't you going to say a little something
over him, Papa? My father hesitated a moment, pulled off his hat,
and then murmured out a few words in the thickening gloom. "In
such an hour as ye know not the Son of Man cometh and we all
got to be ready to go at the last day, blessed be his Holy Name."
But he said nothing about Rassie's being in Heaven, for like a
great many folks in North Carolina at that time he was still a bit
uncertain as to whether Negroes really had full-fledged souls and
would be allowed in Heaven. But I knew that Rassie had gone
straight to Heaven and was right at that moment standing close
by the throne of God and was being petted and taken care of by
the lovely angels gathered round. And when Papa went on home

ahead of me, calling back for me to come on, I drove a sharp little piece of plank down for the headboard. It was good dark now and the evening star was shining close by the frail upturned moon low in the west. I took out the barlow knife and in the gloom carved as best I could a rough cross on the plank. Next day when it was good day-light I would come and cut some words – "Rassie – he sleeps here" – to his memory, real words, yes.

"I'll do it, Rassie," I said aloud. "I'll do it. Rest, Rassie, rest right good," I said.

A long while I stood there, looking down at the grave, the hot tears again scalding my face. Then with swelling, breaking heart I turned and, clutching my precious knife tight in my hand, fol-lowed after my father" (Green, Home to My Valley).

According to Laurence Avery, noted editor, author, and leading expert on Paul Green, to fully see him without interpretation and to really get to know him is to read his letters, written during much of his adult lifetime. Avery, editor of *A Southern Life: Letters of Paul Green, 1916-1981,* actually met Paul Green and received permission to compile this book of letters before Green's passing.

Immersed in Green's letters, both the ones he wrote and the ones he received, one gets a three-dimensional, human snapshot of the real person – not his biography. We see how Green lived and understand his principles and relationships with family and friends. It is apparent through Green's communication that the Hegelian dialectical influence of Horace Williams had swayed his thoughts. Put simply, Hegel's argument rationally explained that a philosopher must know himself before arriving at knowl-edge of the exterior environment.

An Alfred Whitehead or a Plotinus type of pragmatist, Paul Green believed "in truth as a creative process which real men, which important protagonists of our potential dramas can create and sustain, and whose importance and reality lie only in such creativity and such sustaining." He revealed these very intimate thoughts in his response in 1951 to a letter from the very straight talking, then Cornell University doctoral student, Doris Falk.

We get a sense of his love for his life-long mate and literary partner Elizabeth Lay Green.

His letters to "Dear Elizabeth," "Dearest Elizabeth," "Dearest," or some form of the previous greetings seem to be more formal up to the time of their marriage, compared to afterwards. As a single man, he would sometimes playfully greet her very humorously as "Dear Child" or "Dear Girl," etc.

Married, he would greet his wife as "Dear Honey Child," "Dear Honey," "Dear Honey Chile," "Dear Old Gal," (lightheartedly), "Dearest Honey," etc. After matrimony, the beautiful couple would have four children.

Green no doubt expressed his undying love for Elizabeth, often closing with "I love ye." In *A Southern Life,* of 329 total letters that Avery compiled, 61 are written to Elizabeth, the last recorded June 9, 1959.

Green corresponded with several United States governors, and Thomas "Tom" Wolf, Eugene O'Neill, Carl Sandburg, Benjamin Brawley, James "Jim" aka "Squire" Boyd, and a host of others whose presence in Green's life should not be considered lessened because they aren't mentioned here.

To understand Paul Green, the mature adult, and his passion for racial equality and accord, one can look to his childhood and young adulthood experiences. Second Lieutenant Green's experiences in France while serving in the U.S. military during World War I were life changing. Paul loved President Woodrow Wilson's ideas and was eager to enlist in "a war to end war." He sympathized with the French peasants, relating them to many beloved people he knew from rural eastern North Carolina. Their bravery and stability drew him to them.

Despite the military being segregated during Green's tenure, his interaction with African, African–American, and Asian troops on the front lines is believed to have further influenced his viewpoint on race. It was impossible for Green not to notice how the French peasant women genuinely embraced his fellow black soldiers. He observed that this type of casual social behavior was taboo back home for a black man. He further noted that miscegenation, although frowned upon, was considered "sport" when a white man slept with a black woman and produced a child. After returning from France a changed man, Paul Green stated that black men were his equal. This was a remarkable and bold statement for a white male to make in the segregated South at that time in American history.

Green, a member of Phi Beta Kappa, was comfortable with objective criticism of his literary work. A year prior to the premier of the award winning *In Abraham's Bosom*, he corresponded with Mrs. Edith J. R. Isaacs, a white woman, publisher of the renowned magazine *Theatre Arts* and a connoisseur and collector of black culture. He asked Ms. Isaacs for feedback, requesting, "Would you be interested in looking at a play of this length?" Ms. Isaacs informed Green that the play needed to be improved. One can argue that it was her constructive assessment, if received and heeded, that contributed to making the play even better.

In Abraham's Bosom debuted at the Provincetown Theatre in Greenwich Village in New York City as the Harlem Renaissance was into full swing, and a "new psychology" was sweeping the country to an embrace by many whites of nearly anything relating to black culture. It was the era of the famous Cotton Club, which, although segregated (mostly white patrons only), provided exposure for many of the most celebrated black entertainers in the United States. The Harlem Renaissance was also the period where Paul Green was acquainted with intellectuals and literary leaders like Langston Hughes, Zora Neale Hurston, Charles Spearman Johnson, and Arna Bontemps, etc.

Thinking of Green's generosity, I am reminded of "Come Thou Fount of Every Blessing," an old 18th century hymn-poem of the Christian church, and my mother's frequently attempted opera-like rendition of it at home.

"Come thou fount of every blessing tune my heart to sing thy grace.

Streams of mercy never ceasing call for songs of loudest praise…"

My mother had a good heart, and I contend that, as in the British minister and songwriter Robert Robinson's lyrics, Green, who also had a good and loving heart, was in tune, too.

Often my pastor, the lovely and charismatic Reverend Dr. Cynthia L. Hale, has preached to our congregation about giving, mainly as it relates one's heart and the tithe – the giving of 10% of one's income to God. It is hard to argue, for the Bible says in Matthew 6:21 that "For wherever your treasure is, you may be certain that your heart will be there, too." Green knew the Bible very well, had a spirit of giving, and had received numerous blessings over his lifetime. Therefore, he let his life embody the instructions for good living.

Proverbs 27:19 says, "As water reflects a face, so a man's heart reflects the man." When reviewing Green's life, it should be understandable why he felt compelled to give to significant causes, which fought against racial inequality and civil injustice.

Green's empathetic and generous heart caused him to interact with Langston Hughes, one of the most famous American poets, authors, and playwrights of the 20th century, outside the literary realm. Listen to his heart as he writes to Hughes, while living on the west coast in Hollywood, California, in November 1939:

"Dear Langston Hughes:

Like you I have agonized a great deal over the Scotts-boro boys and have contributed what I could both in money and words to their cause, and like you I know that there will never be enough contributions of any kind until these boys are freed. Accordingly I am herewith enclosing a check and the following statement which you, as you request, may release to the press:

For three years now these helpless negro boys have lived in the shadow of death. For three years now the state of Alabama, the South and the nation have failed to discharge their duty to these victims and give them the merciful justice their case demands. If these Scottsboro boys are allowed to be offered up as a sacrifice to bigotry and perverted racial feeling, then we as a Southern people have no right to boast of either democracy or liberty… Thank you

*for writing to me. I shall be back in North Carolina in December
and shall then as now, be ready to do what I can.*

Sincerely yours, "

It is possible that Zora Neale Hurston, writer, folklorist, and anthropologist, connected with Paul Green because she did not portray fellow blacks being victimized in her writings.

"I don't belong to that sobbing school of Negrohood who hold that nature somehow has given them a low down dirty deal," Hurston was once quoted as saying.

Some literary scholars argue that this is due not to naivety but to the influence of her growing up in the independence of Eatonville, a historic all-black rural town just outside of Orlando, Florida. Green understood, close-up, the plight of blacks but wanted his portrayal of them to be more positive. Undoubtedly, Green and the Notasulga, Alabama-born Hurston, as professionals, were closely associated when she taught drama at then North Carolina College, now North Carolina Central University, in Durham during the 1939-1940 school year. While living in the "Bull City" only three years after the release of her most noted work, *Their Eyes Were Watching God,* she attended writing classes on Sunday nights in his Greenwood Road home in Chapel Hill, located about 10 miles away. Hurston and Green, both masters of the Southern rural dialect in their writings, had started, but did not finish, a play with the working title *John de Conqueror.*

Hurston once wrote Green from the low country town of Beaufort, South Carolina, on May 3, 1940, asking for his help. She had been there with fellow Columbia University student of anthropology Frank Boaz, studying life in the black church. Thinking that the fellow student who had gone to New York to obtain filming equipment would return only to capitalize on recording the black spirituals before she could, she anxiously wrote *"Now, don't sit there, Paul Green, just thinking. DO SOMETHING! We cant let all that swell music get away from us like that...Cant you get one of the machines from the University and run a man down here for a week?"*

Later, in early May, Green responded by telegram:

"HAVE ARRANGED FOR SOUND MACHINE BUT IT WOULD COST RATHER HEAVILY TO SEND A MAN AND CAR DOWN THERE COULD YOU DRIVE UP AND GET THEM SINCE I HAVE TO BE IN NEW YORK THE LAST OF NEXT WEEK GOOD GOING AND SO GLAD TO HEAR FROM YOU

PAUL GREEN"

Because Paul Green had acquired racially tolerant social values growing up, it allowed him to collaborate with Richard Wright, a black man, one of America's greatest writers of the 20th century. In 1940-1941, Green worked closely with Wright as he adapted Wright's famous book, *Native Son,* to the Broadway stage. Wright needed Green's experience as a playwright to transition the novel's Bigger Thomas, with his aura of anger, to project a character more compatible with theater during that era. During Wright's visit, he could not stay in the hotels in a pre-integrated Chapel Hill, North Carolina, the town where Green resided. He shared Green's office on campus at the university, thanks to Chancellor Robert House, and his home as workspaces during this collaboration. Wright stayed with several black families in nearby Carrboro while visiting Chapel Hill.

Can you imagine all the scrutiny that "Mr. Green," as Richard Wright respectfully called the playwright, endured as they worked alongside each other in Chapel Hill that hot and humid summer of 1940? Many years later, Green revealed that he was very sensitive to the fact that he and Wright did not address each other on a more personal basis. Green's hindsight suggested that he should have had him "Call me Paul."

Even though Wright and Green had differences of opinion periodically, it was not personal. Their differences were creative. Although Green was very comfortable with people of color, as his actions and his writings would suggest, he and Wright disagreed about the stage portrayal of Bigger Thomas, the main character in *Native Son.* From Green's purview, he thought the portrayal of Bigger Thomas, especially the last scene, should not have portrayed him like a victim. Richard, or "Dick" as Green referred to him, was a lot closer to the play, and he being black or a "Negro" in that era, wanted Bigger's character to maintain true to his race, a perspective that Orson Welles, director of the play, would later share. Wright wanted the viewer to see the social dynamics that contributed to Bigger Thomas' character.

Green shared his viewpoint about *Native Son* in an August 1940 letter, replying to a Methodist pastor from Asheville, North Carolina, who had written to him previously expressing his concern about the planned play based on the novel.

> *"Dear Dr. Stanbury:*
>
> *I appreciate your letter with its kindly advice about the dramatization of the Negro novel, Native Son, and I am hastening to assure you that I, along with you and many another North Carolinian, am most anxious to foster a growing racial accord among our people.*
>
> *... You are right, I think, in feeling that the novel as it now stands has a great deal of bitterness and racial antagonism in it – qualities which are understandable enough. However, there is a basic human truth in the book, and Mr. Wright and I are doing our best to put that truth into the play – a truth shorn of its surrounding hate and evil. I consider the character of Bigger Thomas as depicted in the novel to be a challenge to all right-thinking people. We cannot ignore him. Rather, we should seek to understand him, and the causes which brought him into being...*
>
> *And of course we have to take account of the individual's moral responsibility.*
>
> *With cordial regards."*

What if Charles S. Johnson had not died in 1956? Who was Charles Spurgeon Johnson? Johnson was a leading black sociologist and editor credited as being instrumental to the Harlem Renaissance. Johnson, who eventually became President of Nashville, Tennessee's Fisk University, a post he held until his sudden death in October 1956, had engaged in discussions with Green and renowned black American poet, author, and librarian Arna Bontemps about an outdoor symphonic drama, featuring the Fisk Jubilee Singers and weaving in the impact that black people have had on the culture of America. These talks fizzled upon Johnson's death.

Paul Green admired Reverend Dr. Martin Luther King's "good work of brotherhood and understanding among men." Green was moved and desired to dramatize King's first book, *Stride Toward_Freedom*, his description of the Montgomery bus boycott, which started two years prior. Green had been informed by Harper and Row of their intention to publish King's work. Green informed the publisher, who in turn forwarded his letter to King's literary agent, Marie F. Rodell. Rodell was also a friend and literary agent of Rachel Carson, whose 1962 book, *Silent Spring,* would affect the environmental policy and regulation moving forward in America, if not the world.

> *"Dear Miss Rodell:*
>
> *We are delighted down here in Chapel Hill that Dr. King is on the road to health again. What a terrible thing has happened to him! He has suffered, he has endured, and how wonderful it is that he is still spared…*
>
> *I know that when Dr. King is available I'd like to discuss the matter with him and consider ways and means. Will he be coming back South in this direction anytime within the next few weeks or months?*
>
> *Sincerely yours,"*

King, having returned to Alabama from his stay in a Harlem, New York, hospital, was informed of Green's request through Miss Rodell, who really liked the idea.

King was delighted, telling Green that he "…was certainly happy to hear this and knowing your great reputation in this field my delight was increased even more."

In November 1958, Dr. King and Paul Green twice communicated with each other, with King inviting Green to Montgomery to discuss the project. It was a very racially tense time in America and the Deep South, four years after Brown v. Board of Education of Topeka and with

Montgomery still digesting the searing reality of a hard fought and successful boycott. Green sent his regrets, saying, "My admiration for your fine book is as strong as ever but events have moved in such a way and nature since my first letter to you that I believe a dramatization of it would better wait."

The last time I saw Jesse Helms in person was at my college graduation on May 12, 1980. He received an honorary degree before witnesses on a beautiful sunny Monday morning, on the academic circle in front of Campbell University's D. Rich Building. I knew that the late United States Senator Helms and I had ideological differences politically but he was a friend of the University. He had a very powerful following among conservatives in the Tar Heel State. I had grown up watching his fiery editorials on Raleigh's WRAL-TV, Channel 5.

"What could we possibly have in common besides being native North Carolinians from rural areas?" I had often wondered.

Less than three decades later, I would discover the answer. We both loved Green's book, *Home to My Valley*. Even though "Rassie and the Barlow Knife" is my personal favorite, I can understand why he appreciated "The Corn Shucking," another short story from this same book, published in 1970.

About 10 weeks after my graduation, Helms wrote to Green regarding the non-fiction book, saying that it was "among the most poignant yet entertaining volumes I've ever experienced" and in the same letter inquired curiously about the outcome in the real life love story between Green and the little girl from a farm nearby. Green and Helms were associates, both agreeing and disagreeing on topics of the day and yesteryear. They shared their commonality regarding their love of rural America. They disagreed civilly about nuclear disarmament and America's arms race with Reagan's "Evil Empire," the Soviet Union. Green was pro disarmament and con on the arms race; Helms was ideologically positioned just the opposite.

Four days later, Green in his letter to Helms from Windy Oaks, his residence on Lystra Road, outside of Chapel Hill, wrote the following:

"Dear Jesse:

You are kind and generous in taking time to write me your appreciation of the book of short stories, Home to

My Valley. As to your inquiry about what happened to the girl in "The Corn Shucking," I have to report that the boy went away to the university at Chapel Hill, and in the separation that followed the budding romance between them faded and finally died…it is always great to hear from you. I still remember the frank and pleasant interview we had here some weeks ago under the shade of the maple trees. Best greetings, and warm regards to Mrs. Helms, Paul."

The characters that Green brought to life in his work are real to me. I "feel you," Mr. Green. The modern youthful expression "feel you" sums up how I relate to the characters, setting, and regional essence that he puts into many of his dramatic pieces. Yet, while many of them are fictional, they are known, or so it seems, through my ancestors, former neighbors, farmers, teachers, townspeople, etc. of that era. Better yet, these people characterize many of my kin folks who helped develop and transform the Argyll Colony to what it is today. They, both black and white, may be mere characters to some, but along with their respective settings speak to me and have my ear. I know the people he writes about, yet we have not formally been introduced, obviously. Many of these places, I have seen, although some of the stories may be fictional, formed in the depths of my Southern, rural, childhood memory.

Why should we link Paul Green and ArgyllAmerica, the Spirit? Laurence Avery concedes that Green spent most of his life standing up for the rights of those he felt were disenfranchised. Mr. Green's life can't be simply reduced to a few paragraphs. Nevertheless, the world should know that he stood for things which had significant outcomes in shaping the history of America – prison reform, civil rights of American blacks, and help for Southern textile mill workers in undesirable workplaces. Green was against capital punishment, supported school desegregation (especially following the Supreme Court's Brown vs. Board of Education) and decisions against the Vietnam War, and was for nuclear disarmament.

Avery points out in *A Paul Green Reader* that when Green died, after having lived for some four score and seven years, "it was clear that his life had made a difference in building the New South and had contributed in important ways to North Carolina's growing reputation as the most progressive of southern states."

It was Paul Green who asked "What is the Soul of Man?" Green told us that "Love is the soul of man. "

"Rocka' my soul in the bosom of Abraham
  Rocka' my soul in the bosom of Abraham
  Rocka' my soul in the bosom of Abraham
  Oh, rocka' my soul…"

William Johnson; George McFadden; Phillip Brooks
Heavenly Gospel Singers, 1937 (original recording)

Because of Green's values and his generous heart, I will always believe that "the cotton picker" is a reflection of ArgyllAmerica.

4

Tobacco Road

"Let me tell you about the tobacco roads in my life"
- The Author

Although Georgia is the setting in Erskine Caldwell's 1932 novel *Tobacco Road*, it vicariously became an expression with North Carolina roots. Many a modern sportsman has heard about "Tobacco Road," a reference made famous regarding four North Carolina universities affiliated with the Atlantic Coast Conference (ACC) who share close proximity to U.S. Interstate 40.

Duke University, N.C. State University, and University of North Carolina at Chapel Hill share an area called the Research Triangle Park (RTP), while Wake Forest University makes the Triad area of North Carolina its home. Wake was once located in Wake Forest, North Carolina, near Raleigh, before relocating west to its campus in Winston-Salem in 1956. R.J. Reynolds gave Wake a large amount of tobacco money to move the 110 miles west through the Piedmont region on I-40. Before then, the schools, all located within a 34-mile radius, established simmering hot basketball rivalries. The words *Tobacco Road* have become an established marketing brand, etched in the minds of sports fans.

Being an avid sports fan and a native North Carolinian means that I, like thousands of others in the state, LOVE basketball. *Tobacco Road* and the Greensboro Coliseum are synonymous words in this basketball-crazed state. My priceless early childhood memories include watching on TV David "Skywalker" Thompson and number one ranked N.C. State's overtime win over a very talented Maryland team for the 1974 ACC Championship.

It was conference winner take all back then – do or die. It saddened fans and frustrated the NCAA to see fourth-ranked Maryland go home so early. The Terrapins felt that playing in the NIT, though very respectful, was not worthy of their caliber ball club and season. The consensus among losing Coach Lefty Driesell's players was that "we just played for the national championship."

Finally, two weeks later on the same floor, State's not so surprising semifinal upset of Bill Walton's John Wooden-coached UCLA team in the Final Four was the cherry on top for many basketball enthusiasts such as I. The Wolfpack, coached by Norm Sloan, would go on to defeat Marquette in the national championship game, 76-64.

The next year, the NCAA expanded the tournament. Many people speculated that the ACC battle the previous year led to the well-deserved change, giving more than one outstanding team in major conferences an opportunity to succeed. Therefore, a highly talented team such as Maryland, which had several All-Americans, would not risk feeling penalized if they failed to win their conference tournament. Likewise, a regular season champion from a major conference could still move on, despite the possibility of being upset in the same tourney.

More intimate memories along this *Tobacco Road* conjure up summers past in the 1970s and the many pilgrimages to the North Carolina High School East vs. West All Star Basketball game. My youngest brother Herbert and I would excitedly ride to Greensboro with our second oldest brother Warren, aka "Hawk" or "PeeWee," during the early afternoon of game day. We would arrive at 1703 Lincoln Street in the Gate City at the home of my mother's oldest sister, Lula Bell Clark Rooks, and her proud husband Paul. Uncle Rooks was a retired transplanted Midwesterner from Kansas City, who had worked his way up through the ranks of the military as an unlisted man to become a sergeant. They loved our short summer overnight visits to their home and were most hospitable. We'd cut the grass and do any other chores that needed to be done before eating one of Aunt Bell's delicious meals and heading off to West Lee Street for the game.

July 30, 1974, will always be a signature date for my younger brother Herbert and me along this famous road. We had decent seats and were sitting in the lower level of the arena in Section 128, Row F, when we struck up a conversation with a white gentleman sitting next to us. He said he was a friend of Dean Smith's, head basketball coach for the North Carolina Tar Heels.

Herbert and I were both Carolina fans, but this was the "year of the Wolfpack" in the ACC and the nation. Herbert maintained his loyalty and wore his bright powder blue high top Chuck Taylors®. I did the unthinkable! I was a bit more fair-weather this particular season, swayed by the success story of high-flying Thompson, mountain 'giant of a man' Tommy Burleson, and diminutive point guard Monte Towe. Proudly, I wore my white Wolfpack T-shirt.

The gentleman, whose name has long been forgotten, said that he was going down near courtside to see Coach Smith at half time.

"Can we go with you?" Herbert asked, like the little kid he was.

I looked at my brother as if chastising him for being so forward, but at the same time hoping that our newfound friend would say yes.

Coach Smith, who was there to see All-American point guard Phil Ford, his prized incoming recruit from Rocky Mount, North Carolina, warmly greeted us. After briefly chatting with his friend, he looked down to my brother's feet, smiled, and said, "I like the color of your tennis shoes." He then looked at me and gave me one of those playful grins, as if to say, "What are you doing wearing that shirt?" It was kind of an awkward moment for a second, but we all shook hands and parted. My excitement at having met one of the most respected coaches in the nation, an opportunity envied by many teenagers my age, easily overshadowed any circumstance. It obviously was an inspiring moment for Herbert, as well – one that, along with talent and dedication, afforded him the opportunity to play on the very same floor and in the same event six years later.

As an adult, I would eventually understand Coach Smith's passion for civil rights and the impact he made on advancing race relations in Chapel Hill, North Carolina, and the university. Many basketball enthusiasts know that it was he who first integrated the UNC basketball program when New York City hoopster Charlie Scott became the first African-American on scholarship. Smith was also very involved in ensuring that many local businesses treated blacks fairly.

However, there are many tobacco roads in ArgyllAmerica which have nothing to do with sports, prestigious universities, or an interstate highway. While the Old North State is still the nation's top producer of tobacco, many farmers no longer continue the tradition of their ancestors and have focused on other top producing commodities, such as broilers and hogs, or have left the profession altogether. In fact, in this region, what used to be farms often give way to subdivisions and shopping centers.

Let me tell you about the tobacco roads in my life.

I never was a smoker. Okay, I tried to smoke a cigarette once but could not get past my gasping for air as the smoke nearly choked me to death. Interestingly enough, the smell of flue-cured tobacco in a rustic tin-roofed barn drifting into the air beside a two-lane country road conjures up warm memories formed long ago.

Photo: Old Tobacco Barn on Hwy 27
Lillington, NC

The tobacco road I know is a thoroughfare that reveals a certain resilient work ethic created over several centuries among farmers, many of whom were descendants of early Gaelic-speaking Scottish immigrants, and workers, often, but not always, African-Americans generations removed from slavery. Tobacco, curing in a barn, represented to some a collective body of work. To the farmers, it represented their livelihood – a step closer to market and an eventual payday.

Likewise, for most workers, tobacco leaves curing in a barn was a reflection of their final point in the process – a contribution made and honest pay for honest work. Many life lessons were learned while toiling the tobacco roads once known as the Argyll Colony.

At one point in U.S. history, my tobacco roads might have been one of the few places where both black and white had roles that at least gave the illusion of being equal. My tobacco road is where values such as accountability and determination mold the psyche of people in the region. This is a typical summer day, as I recall, along my tobacco road:

Wake-up came early. It was 4:30 in the morning. The alarm sounded, but I had been awake at least 30 minutes. I couldn't sleep thinking about the work ahead. Soon, Brian would be pulling up in the yard to pick us up. Daddy poked his head into the room to see if we actually were awake and getting dressed. Earning our own spending money was a critical part of the family's financial equation, and daddy counted on his children's independence during the summer months. My brother Herbert and I had mixed emotions about going to work, as we dreaded what the actual day would bring. Yet, we looked forward to the monetary reward it would bring at the end of our workday.

Five o'clock a.m. came and our ride arrived. We heard the sound of the truck's muffler as it came down the driveway through the darkness. "Beep Beep! Beep Beep!" as Brian blew his horn. Herbert and I approached the truck. The two extra seats in the cab were not available.

The truck had no canopy. All the choice locations on the truck bed which minimized the impact of the cool moist incoming wind would already be taken. We took positions in any available space, making sure our heads were tucked or using someone's body to shield us from the rush of moist morning air.

Shortly after boarding the truck, we arrived at the tobacco farm and waited to catch a ride to the "field of choice" that day. Two wooden trailers with low-cut sides connected to the red John Deere™ tractor. We hopped on the trailers and braced ourselves for the bumpy, dusty ride to our destination.

At 5:30 a.m., I stood in front of my tobacco row – my official starting point for the day. Sunrise was yet a half-hour away, but there was just enough light to see what we needed to do. I tried not to look at the enormity of the field that lay in front of me – only a glance. It seemed to me that giving it a quick look-over somehow reduced the size of the challenge.

Then Brian, the farmer's son and field team leader, shouted, "Let's go!" The cool drops of morning dew on the huge bright green tobacco leaves touched my face – my entire body - each time I "primed" a leaf, sending shivers through me. Priming, or harvesting as some refer to it, involves the removal of ripened yellow-green colored leaves on the tobacco stalk. Soon, my clothes, from my hat to my shoes, would be wet, dripping a mixture of sweat, dew, and tobacco juice on the ground. My shoes squished each time I walked from my row to the trailer to unload the leaves filling my arms. We greeted a beautiful sunrise, and our connection with nature and the God above seemed as one. I was tired already but dared not admit it publicly, for I had my job to do. We, in that field, black and white, were all brothers determined to make it – to grind through it. We were accountable, and many people were depending on us to produce.

Soon it was mid-morning and "Old Joshua" was beaming down on us as it rose in the eastern sky. I'm not quite sure where we picked up the expression "Old Joshua," but it was probably in church or listening to the old-timers. Joshua 10:13 of the NIV says, "…The sun stopped in the middle of the sky and delayed going down about a full day." All I know is that "Old Joshua" refers to the sun. My back ached from the constant bending over to grasp leaves around the lowest part of the stalk, called sandlugs. The dark tobacco sap had dried and become a sticky pitch tar as the temperature climbed even higher. Before, we had to deal with the cool morning dew. Now, the sandy soil picked up from the leaves around the ground covered my body and was imbedded in the tar.

At last, it was break time and my fatigued body couldn't agree more. The tobacco primers were glad to see the tractor driver as he brought another empty trailer because we knew that on board were our well-deserved snacks. Brian yelled, "Break time!" but it was never more obvious. We all lined up to choose a Pepsi-Cola or Mountain Dew and a "nab." "Nab" is the colloquial word for a peanut butter cracker. There was no bottled water; that would not become fashionable for a few more decades. Aah! The trailer carried a cooler of ice water to quench our thirst.

With a Pepsi and a pack of nabs in hand, I looked for any available shade. I found cover under a mature longleaf pine, checking first for the possibility of snakes or an ant mound that might be nearby. As I rested, I spied a big green tobacco worm clinging to my left shirtsleeve and quickly flicked it off. It must have been at least 90 º, and it was not even 10 a.m. "Old Joshua" was unrelenting. I prayed that this was a short workday but overheard Brian telling the tractor driver that we just might work that afternoon. Slowly, we edged our way back toward our tobacco rows.

Brian, being the leader he was, called "Let's go!" with his persuasive Carolina twang.

An hour passed before word finally arrived from Brian's dad, back at the barn. He told Brian we needed three more rounds before completely filling the barn. At that time, we would stop for the day because of the oppressive heat and humidity. We would complete the field and start filling a new barn early in the morning.

Oh! Thank you, God! You were listening. Suddenly, it seemed as if we had gained strength. Even Brian was pleasantly surprised. Fatigue? What back pain? The sun? Who's "Old...?" Well, we'd leave that alone. We knew we would want "Old Joshua" to be good to us tomorrow. Brian's father was a reasonable man. He knew that continuing after lunch might have caused Brian and all the primers to have over exposure to the sun. He could count on us being back tomorrow. Hell, the primers all needed the money. It might have been nice if we had received a full day's pay, but leaving in good health was more important. We were all happy because day's end was near. I began to softly hum Don McLean's chart buster:

*"Bye, bye, Miss American Pie,
Drove my Chevy to the levee but the levee was dry.
Them good ol' boys were drinkin' whiskey 'n' rye.
Singin' this will be the day that I die.
This will be the day that I die."*

I continued to hum the same part of the song repeatedly for at least another five minutes. Then, in a more energetic fashion, I broke out singing, still at a low volume, with Billy Preston and Bruce Fisher's hit:

*"Nothin' from nothin' leaves nothin'
You gotta have somethin'*

71

If you wanna be with me
Nothin' from nothin' leaves nothin'
You gotta have somethin'
If you wanna be with me."

These two songs helped me to entertain myself by passing the time and by taking my mind off the conditions, if only shortly. It also allowed me to realize that I could appreciate a diversity of music because it was everybody's music to enjoy.

Having completed the third and final round, we hopped on the trailer, making sure not to sit on the tobacco leaves. I barely noticed the ruts in the private dirt road caused by erosion over the years. The dust being kicked up by the big tractor tires and smaller trailer tires did not seem to bother anyone, either.

Now at the barn, we saw the workers, mostly women, emptying the remaining trailers, as they wrapped or "looped" the big tobacco leaves to long wooden rectangular sticks, using twine. Some of us, hoping to speed things up, volunteered to help where possible, becoming "handers." We looked into the barn to speak to the men "hanging" the full tobacco sticks. They were shirtless and sweat popped off their bodies; it felt like a sauna inside. The men were close to finishing out the barn. We knew that we were done when all the work at the barn was finished.

Work was complete for most of us. A sense of pride overwhelmed us. Brian looked at the primers, smiled, and repeated his oft spoken words, "Let's go!" Even though we were not returning to work, we still were hungry and needed nourishment. We traveled a few miles to the Olivia Trading Post, which had a grill. This was a very popular lunch spot.

The Trading Post was located in a rural community, originally named Rock Branch, founded in 1865, the same year the Civil War ended. Grateful to W. S. Olive for introducing flue-cured tobacco to the area, its name was changed to Olivia in 1913. It was here, seeing all the other farm workers coming in and out, that we realized we were not the only people with a work ethic. It was obvious that many were working in tobacco, as well, because our clothes looked the same. We all had sandy shoes and clothes that were a grimy looking green and black, imbedded with gummy sticky tar. Even though we did not know everyone by name, and only occasionally nodded as we passed each other in the store, we shared common values. An unspoken thought prevailed among us: "If we can do this (tobacco), we can do anything."

As we traveled down the two-lane blacktop back home, I looked at the beautiful countryside and reflected on my life on tobacco road. I realized that my experience was only a subset of what Brian's family lived. Their experience started well before the sandlugs were even primed and encompassed much more than priming a field to fill a barn, in preparation for curing the leaves. Before any of us ever set foot on the farm, they had planted the tobacco seedlings and topped the sickles.

After the tobacco leaves are flue-cured and removed from the barn, they are placed in large bundles and ultimately trucked to market in places like Wilson or Rocky Mount. Most of the primers knew nothing of the details of this part of the process, unless we had worked on a relative's small tobacco farm. As others were dropped off before Herbert and me, they said goodbye for the day, in a manner almost congratulatory. We felt blessed to be able to clean-up, rest, and seek shelter from "Old Joshua."

We began to smile gleefully as Brain pulled down the long gray sandy driveway to our home. He said, "I appreciate it. See you tomorrow morning." Herbert and I nodded and began pulling off our grimy shirts as we headed to the outside water faucet by the well.

Like many people who grew up in the American South, the tobacco roads of my life were a place that engrained a spirit of resilience, connection to and appreciation for nature, and mutual respect between the races. If, and when, one has gained an appreciation for these values, which are the essence of my tobacco road, they have discovered ArgyllAmerica.

5

Campbell University

"Cam beul": Gaelic, *meaning curved mouth*

ArgyllAmerica has indeed found Campbell, or should I say that J.A. Campbell's 12 decades plus grown-up academy has found it. The spirit of racial and cultural diversity was being manifested in Assistant Athletic Director for Marketing and Promotions Kevin Lyle's choice of half-time programming, music and dance, at the Jacksonville University Men's basketball game. Even more important, the response from the students and most of the fans served as confirmation.

My former basketball teammate my sophomore and junior years, 6'8" Roddney McCants, his wife Valerie, and my cousin James Johnson, Jr., were sitting in the orange seats in Section 110 of Campbell's new John W. Pope, Jr. Convocation Center, engaged in conversation, when the influence of the youthful Cupid himself, Bryson Bernard, came front and center on the playing floor below.

The *Cupid Shuffle*, a nation-wide hit by the Lafayette, Louisiana-born multiple-octave-range vocalist, burned up the airwaves in 2007, and was being played as part of the half-time entertainment. Dozens of students, black and white, joined the cheerleaders and got down to the song, while energetically doing the popular line dance made famous by the former church choir member and son of a pastor.

I instantly started bobbing my head, proud of the cultural diversity that my conservative alma mater was displaying. I looked to my cousin and said emphatically, "I love it!"

> *"Down, down, do your dance, do your dance*
> *Down, down, do your dance, do your dance*
> *Down, down, do your dance, do your dance*
> *Down, down, do your dance, do your dance"*

Roddney and I looked at each other shortly, with a little grin, which seemed to say to me that "man, times have really changed…for the better."

> *"To the right, the right, the right, the right, the right*
> *The left, the left, the left, the left, the left*
> *Now kick, now kick, now kick, now kick*
> *Now walk it by yourself, now walk it by yourself."*

By now, I have literally moved to the edge of my seat, swaying to the dips, kicks, and turns made by the youthful, energetic dance participants below to the *Cupid Shuffle.*

THE PRESIDENTS

Reverend Dr. J.A. Campbell (JAC)

The Spirit of ArgyllAmerica can't be rationally explained. It causes the paths of many people to cross which might not otherwise. For example, it is a well-known fact that a white man, James Archibald (J.A.) Campbell, a descendant of Scottish immigrants, founded what is now Campbell University, in 1887. Documented in J. Winston Pearce's book, *Campbell College: Big Miracle at Little_Buies Creek,* but not as well known, is the importance that other races and cultures played in his early spiritual development. One such passage from this magnificent book lends support:

"The son, James Archibald Campbell, had a high and firm allegiance to

Jesus Christ as the Lord and Master of his life. It is necessary to keep this in mind or there will be no real understanding of the man or what he did. From the night when a man, who happened to have black skin, turned the boy's life toward Jesus to the day when he died with his face bathed in the sunlight, James Archibald Campbell was a possessed man – possessed by Jesus Christ and his way of life." (J. Winston Pearce, Campbell College: Big Miracle at Little Buies Creek).

Campbell University Entrance on Dr. Leslie Hartwell Campbell Drive

This insight brings forth the fact that J.A. Campbell, like Paul Green, and their families had close ties with blacks in the Upper Cape Fear Valley. This had to be the case for what is arguably the single most important experience in his life, led to Christ by a descendant of slaves, not a white preacher or believer. That experience would eventually impact the establishment of the second largest private university in the state of North Carolina, but more importantly, influence the lives of thousands of young men and women through the all-around Christian education experience and effect change in its community, state, nation…and world.

Reverend Campbell embodied the resiliency principle of ArgyllAmerica. North Carolina native son Paul Green once described the first school president as having a "high forehead, classical facial lines, trim moustache, and elegant wire-rim reading glasses, Campbell looked the part that he was, that is, a tough, intelligent, pragmatic, and resilient administrator."

Dr. Leslie Hartwell Campbell (LHC)
"We Will Work It Out Some Way!"

Dr. Leslie Hartwell Campbell (LHC), the son of Dr. J.A. Campbell, was unanimously elected by the Board of Trustees as president of the college in March 1934. He assumed the almost overwhelming responsibility of leading the school his father founded, with a heavy heart. Upon his father's passing, Dr. Leslie Hartwell Campbell did not have much time to grieve as it was the era of the Great Depression and he had to find a way to sustain the legacy his father started late in the 19th century.

In the fall of 1934, the new Campbell president, Dr. Leslie Hartwell Campbell, with his big grin, welcomed new students in a speech captured by the school newspaper, *Creek Pebbles*, titled "Third Crisis in it he stated:

> *"You are here to witness the third crisis in the history of our school. The first came when the entire school plant was destroyed by fire in 1900. The second was the transition from an academy to a junior college. The third came when the founder-president died last spring. Each time friends and curious on-lookers wondered if the school could carry on. Both times it has before, and we trust that it shall now so long as it cherishes and clings firmly to the Christian ideals of its founder."*

A favorite teacher was Catherine King. She had a beautiful spirit and one could easily see godliness in her actions. I enjoyed taking her class "Man in the Home" during my final semester. Put simply, it was a home economics class for men. We learned very practical things like budgets, money management, and the pros and cons of housing options, etc.

What I remember most about the Tuesday and Thursday morning class was the day we took a field trip to nearby Keith Hills Golf Course to identify residential architecture. She had prepared us well, educating us on the various home styles.

Mrs. King was very humble. Little did I know then that she was *Catherine Campbell King* - Dr. Leslie Hartwell Campbell's oldest daughter and second oldest child, born during his second marriage. She was so humble that I don't remember her talking about that relationship with her students in my class. Perhaps many of my fellow classmates already knew. I respect Mrs. King even more today, several decades later. Sometimes we learn much about a person from the people closest to them – their family.

Catherine Campbell King wrote the following in 1992, one hundred years after the anniversary of her father's birth and twenty-two years after his passing:

Memories of Life With Father

"...*Daddy was, indeed, the head of the family although mother assumed most of the responsibility for child rearing and homemaking. Growing up in a patriarchal family himself, daddy continued the tradition by pretty much setting the economic, social, educational, and spiritual standards by which we lived...*

One of the faculty members who meant so much to Daddy was Dr. M.L. Skaggs, a learned history professor and an amateur golfer; it was he who brought the game of golf to Buie's Creek and got Daddy, Dean Burkot, and other men really "hooked" on the game...

...I really came to appreciate his dedication to Campbell and the sacrificial way in which he put his responsibility to the

people with whom he worked and came in contact above personal gain. I was impressed with his love and concern for others – regardless of their role or status. His interest in the students who were conscientious about getting an education was shown in his personal efforts to make their dreams a reality. His interest in sharing his home with family and friends – whether it was an invitation to a watermelon-cutting - was such a big part of his warm personality.

Daddy heartily endorsed my choice of husband, Bob King; and he thoroughly enjoyed our two daughters, Kathy and Beth. When Kathy was about eleven and Beth about nine, Daddy sent a recommendation to the Admissions Office at Campbell saying that they were good prospects for admission. He would have been so proud to see Beth receive her degree in trust management from this beloved institution...

...I am still influenced by the Christian principles which his life so well exemplified, by his love for learning and personal development, and by the heritage which he gave me."

Dr. Leslie Hartwell Campbell 's career as the leader of Campbell spanned part or all of four different decades and required action on a lot of major issues that resulted because of cultural and civil societal changes and America's involvement in global conflict or war.

President Leslie Hartwell Campbell exhibited courage, empathy, and great foresight. For example, in a tribute to blacks in a 1939 chapel program themed "An Appreciation of the Negro Race," Dr. Leslie Hartwell Campbell, who employed a black nanny and cook named Ada, spoke of the gratitude of whites to blacks, saying that he would suggest to name

"the meanest person in this school. It's not the person who will rob the college, but the one who would cheat a washer-wom-

*an out of her hard-earned nickels for scrubbing clothes. I'm afraid
our school community suffers more from theft among the white
folks than the black. We'd feel safe in leaving everything in our
house unlocked if Ada or Jesse, our colored servants, were the only
ones there. We feel safe in leaving our small children in their care,"*

Dr. LAC said emphatically, with great passion. Immediately after speaking, he and three others together sang Negro spirituals.

According to *Creek Pebbles*, the school newspaper, in early 1940, during chapel, Dr. Leslie Hartwell Campbell announced the following:

*"...that in view of the expense involved in maintaining
inter-collegiate football, the administration had reached the decision to discontinue football, at least for the coming year...If at the
end of another year, it seems good to revert to football, we shall not
hesitate to reinstate it."*

Creek Pebbles reported further that many of Dr. Leslie Hartwell Campbell 's associates stated that Campbell, a sports enthusiast, was the college's major proponent of football, adding that the *"decision to abolish football was to him, personally, a sad step to take but one he deemed wise and practical."*.

Coach Earl Smith, the highly successful football coach during that era, was notified that Campbell might not want to play the Camp Lejeune team they were scheduled to play, since the Camp Lejeune team had black ball players. A man of integrity, Smith asked his team. Not one player objected. This game, played in 1948, will go down in Campbell history as the "man's a man for a' that" game because of the spirit of respect in which Campbell's players are reported to have played against the marines.

So impressed was Camp Lejeune's base commanding officer, he wrote to President Campbell several days later congratulating the squad "on their fine attitude toward every man on the Lejeune team."

Campbell would continue to struggle with supporting football, eventually stopping after the 1950 season. Coach Smith, with his single wing offense and numerous defenses, stated that

> *"Football was discontinued in 1950 because the school couldn't afford it. At the time the school had two major financial drains, a farm that grew food to feed the 300 students and the football program."*

Campbell reinstated their inter-collegiate football program against Birmingham – Southern on August 30, 2008, with the 91-year old Smith on the sidelines in his motorized wheelchair. He and several former members helped to cheer the fighting Camels on, as they lost to the Panthers, 12-6, before a crowd of 5,845 people. It was the largest attendance ever for a Campbell home sporting event.

In Chicago, forty years prior, immediately after news of King's death, rioting broke out and fires burned on the West Side of the city as three thousand National Guard troops were initially deployed. By Saturday, riots had also broken out in Baltimore and more than 100 American cities. Complicating the minds and hearts of many citizens even before the tragic day of King's murder was the Vietnam War. We were a divided nation. While people gathered in Buies Creek to witness the inauguration, President Lyndon Baines Johnson was on the phone at the White House, spending much of his time monitoring the riots and meeting with General William Westmoreland and several of his top advisors to discuss the war.

On April 4, 1968, the reflective mood of America was mixed because of Dr. Martin Luther King's assassination in Memphis two days earlier. Many were sad because King, a Nobel Peace Prize winner, preacher, and charismatic leader of the civil rights movement, had been murdered in cold blood as he stood on the balcony of the Lorraine Hotel. Painfully sad, but true, some Americans were happy to see the young King "put in his place" permanently, perhaps thinking that the movement which had gained momentum during the 1960s would be stalled or dissolved.

There was a slight rain during the day Saturday, April 6, about ¼ of an inch. Otherwise, it was a fresh, warm spring day. It was inauguration day and transition time between the second and third presidents.

In "The Creek," it was a significant time, a formal passing of power that had only taken place once before in the school's history. As Dr. Leslie Hartwell Campbell presented incoming president Dr. Norman A. Wiggins with the presidential medallion, he quoted three lines from Tennyson's "Morte D'Arthur":

> *"The old order changeth, yielding place to new,*
> *And God fulfils himself in many ways*
> *Lest one good custom should corrupt the world."*

Possibly considered even more moving are the next seven lines, which Dr. Leslie Hartwell Campbell did not continue to recite to Wiggins. In Lord Alfred Tennyson's Morte D'Arthur, Lord Arthur, replying to Sir Bedivere's rhetorical cry, continues to speak as he answers slowly from the barge:

> *"Comfort thyself: what comfort is in me?*
> *I have lived my life, and that which I have done*
> *May He within Himself make pure! but thou,*
> *If thou shouldst never see my face again,*
> *Pray for my soul. More things are wrought by prayer*
> *Than this world dreams of. Wherefore, let thy voice*
> *Rise like a fountain for me night and day."*

In kindest expression near the end of his life, Dr. Leslie Hartwell Campbell, the father, wrote to his eldest son Hartwell, after returning from a joint family trip to Florida, *"It is wonderful to be loved and appreciated."*

Dr. Norman Adrian Wiggins (NAW), Class of 1948

"I'm going to miss you, dear friend."

Dr. Wiggins was Campbell's third president, assuming the reigns from Dr. Leslie Hartwell Campbell. It is both ironic and interesting that Dr. Wiggins succeeded the second Dr. Campbell upon his retirement in 1967. Twenty-five years earlier, the two men met for the first time when

Ernest R. Gilchrist

Wiggins, eighteen years old and a prospective student, spent a weekend in Buies Creek in late summer. To his and friend Ervin's surprise, they were invited to breakfast at President and Mrs. Ora Lee Green Campbell's home. Wiggins would write nearly 50 years later about this act of kindness extended to him and his childhood friend.

We Will Work It Out Some Way!

Upon graduation from Burlington high school in 1942, I came to believe that I would be awarded an athletic scholarship to attend Campbell College. Having heard nothing from the school, I decided to visit the campus. Accompanied by the late Ervin Sykes, my classmate and boyhood friend of Burlington, our hometown, we journeyed to the campus on a hot August afternoon. School was out, so activity in the "Creek" was not great. We found that the coach had left to enter the armed forces. A new coach, the late S.O. Brandon, was just moving into what would, many years later, become Marshbanks House. The cafeteria was closed.

Two wonderful women gave Ervin and me a much-needed and greatly appreciated sandwich. Late in the evening, President Campbell returned to campus and came over to the faculty annex (now Layton Annex where the English Department is located) to invite us to his house for a Sunday morning breakfast. Although we would not be properly dressed for the occasion, we accepted the invitation and dreamed of breakfast. It had been a long time since we had had a good meal.

President and Mrs. Campbell graciously greeted us upon our arrival for breakfast. The meal was wonderful and when it was over, there were no leftovers to be put away.

President Campbell and I had a long talk. Yes, he had

heard about me. Yes, my scholarship was secure. Yes, they would be looking for me in September.

The time came for us to leave. We graciously and gratefully thanked Mrs. Campbell for the delicious breakfast. As we were about to leave the porch, I turned to President Campbell and asked that I might see him for just a moment. When alone, I said, "I believe that I should tell you that because of the illness of my father, I do not have any money except what I have earned working this summer in the Sykes Foundry and Machine Shop.

President Campbell stepped back and with that warm friendly smile for which he was known, said, "I wouldn't worry about that. Nobody has any money down here. We will work it out some way."

It was a memorable weekend. But it wasn't easy convincing my mother and father that Ervin and I had had Sunday morning breakfast with the president of Campbell and his wife."

History will remember Dr. Wiggins for many things. He was the first non-Campbell descendant to become president and served 36 years. The establishment of Campbell's Norman Adrian Wiggins School of Law and the School of Pharmacy may lead the legacy, but certainly doesn't minimize the formation and growth of its Schools of Business, Education, and Divinity, which occurred under his watch.

Three things stand out in my personal reflections, which are quite simple and not intended to understate the magnitude of his legacy. His support for the Campbell Men's basketball team in Kansas City, Missouri, during the National Association of Intercollegiate Athletics (NAIA) Tourney was memorable, as he showed his ambassadorship as our leader.

Another footprint moment came when Wiggins subbed for Mr. Marshall Woodall, my Business Law professor, the day of the big snowstorm in 1978, when many teachers could not make it to class. We were about one minute from running out the back door of the classroom in D. Rich Building when he appeared. Imagine, the president of the college "filling in" for your absent professor on a hazardous and snowy day.

Lastly, his parting words at graduation to me were, "I'm going to miss you, dear friend." Of course, he must have repeated the same words hundreds of times as graduates accepted their diplomas, but with his firm handshake, arm fully extended and eyes locked on mine, it seemed customized for me.

Dr. Jerry M. Wallace (JMW)
"Religion – it was a rope, not a thread!"

President Jerry Wallace's moral fiber is as resilient and grounded as the strength of the textiles produced in the warm and sticky Rockingham, North Carolina, mill where he labored for many summers during his undergraduate years. According to Dr. Wallace, his family came from Moore County, NC. Proud of his heritage, he shared that his great-grandfather was killed in the Battle of Sharpsburg in 1862. Wallace grew up with brothers Mitchell and William Wallace, Jr. in a working class household, gaining strength through adversity. Having witnessed his mother go to work to support the family when his dad became ill, he remembered his youth vividly. Dr. Wallace recalls his childhood as being part of a "family struggling, a family that cooperated, and a family that depended on the larger extended family."

Dr. Wallace stated that his youthful memories of the Sandhills are of "a good place because of the church, Rockingham High School, athletics, and a strong family tradition."

"The good Lord looked down upon this day and smiled," said Dr. Wallace, a descendant of Scottish immigrants, as he, with a beaming face, looked up towards Heaven before glancing around at the young men gathered on the porch of Marshbanks Dining Hall.

Standing outside the dining hall after Sunday dinner that sunny afternoon in the late 1970s were several student-athletes. Carlton Thompson, the Heckstall brothers, and I were passing time by people watching, especially the ladies. Dr. Wallace, then the Chairman of the Department of Religion and Philosophy as well as the Tyner Professor of Religion, was a very likable, down to earth person.

"Yes sir," we collectively remarked, as everyone nodded in agreement.

"There is something different about Dr. Wallace besides being friendly," I thought, but I could not put my finger on it – then.

Now president of the University since 2003, he is leading Campbell's "quest to fully implement the Campus Master Plan." With the addition of Starbucks, Chick-fil-A, Quiznos, and Barnes and Noble, now part of the campus offerings, Campbell's physical transition has been most striking under his leadership. This includes a new convocation center, residence hall, pharmacy teaching facility, football stadium, and chapel, along with the renovation of several key buildings on campus. On the drawing board or in various stages of construction is a baseball stadium and track and field venue. He has provided leadership, which has seen the re-activation of Campbell's football program, eliminated shortly after World War II.

Campbell University and it previous presidents have a strong history. When asked in a 2011 interview how he has benefited from their legacy, he stated that "their achievement, integrity, vision and sacrifice" were critical.

"The presidents of Campbell have not moved on when they struggled and were committed to a strong social compass," he added.

Understanding ArgyllAmerica is to value the outdoors – the Cape Fear River, the loneleaf pine, and the Sandhills. President Wallace, after reflecting on the statement, shared his thoughts about his appreciation for Campbell's proximity to its environment.

"Campbell is an academic institution located in a rural area. We live in an area not surrounded by city blocks. The location of its campus is close to nature." Wallace noted, "When I think of the relationship between God and nature, it reminds me of His continual creation and care for us."

How has Campbell's presence in the greater community been felt? Dr. Wallace stated that as an educational university, because of Campbell increasingly multicultural student body, it "will make students more inclusive…more embracing."

He was thankful, he said, that Campbell "was faithful to its founding purpose, which was to be a distinct Christian school, which became an academy, junior college, college, university, and presently a university that is expanding and growing."

As with most school leaders, wisdom is a virtue. President Wallace told parting students at Campbell's 2010 graduation that "a life of getting and spending without a life of giving and service is a dead end." Wallace says, "Faith. Learning. Service. Hands down, it's what Campbell is all about."

THINGS REMEMBERED

Thoughts of Campbell remind me of peaceful early Saturday morning walks across campus to Marshbanks for breakfast, through the academic circle with its historic Kivett Hall and old well, along well-maintained red brick paved sidewalks and well-manicured lawns. With the smells of bacon and sausage filling the air before my arrival, I had a feeling of ownership because the campus was often quiet, except for the bell clock chiming.

Photo: Kivett Hall, Campbell University, Buies Creek, NC

I am not alone, as this is also the memory of another former Campbell graduate. John Beldon, Campbell University class of 1984, wrote the following:

Following the Red Brick Sidewalks

Perhaps my fondest memories of my days at Campbell came from my many walks across campus, the grassy activity fields, the causeways between buildings, the red brick paths. I have an affinity for walking and thinking and, I am told by acquaintance, I also have a proclivity for hanging my head as I do. I plead guilty to this unattractive habit. I do not do it, so far as I am consciously aware, for reasons of low self-esteem or anti-social sentiments; however, being lost in thought and succumbing to the force of gravity mate chin with breastbone.

Returning from meetings or classes, even at night, I would notice, eyes to the earth, the soothing symmetry of the carefully laid brick paths under foot. Those beautiful red bricks. To this day I am amazed that no destruction came to the walkways during my four years as a student, astonished that they had held up so well under what looked like a minimum of maintenance. The university was even able to add a host of small brick tributaries to the existing major pathways, installed with such natural ease and quickness and propriety that one suspected these, the added brickways, were there from the beginning.

Dr. Donald Keyser's Religion 101 Class in Taylor Hall and the day he explained Proverbs 18:24 stand out among what seemed like countless days spent there. Even at age 18, in my progression from adolescence to young adulthood, the scripture seemed to move me.

"Let's examine it together," as Keyser had learned from his former Sunday School class teacher and school president Dr. Leslie Hartwell Campbell.

"A man that hath friends must shew himself friendly: and there is a friend that sticketh closer than a brother," said a balding Dr. Keyser, reading through his rim glasses from his King James Version of the Bible.

Dr. Keyser was very engaging, probing into the scripture, as an excellent theologian should. Like President Leslie Campbell before him, Keyser also believed in class participation and thought that a student's understanding of the scripture enhanced his own.

Thomas (Tom) Harold Folwell was simply the best. Part marketing professor, part country farmer, Mr. Folwell was as comfortable tilling the soil as he was in the classroom explaining "the marketing mix," the 4 Ps of marketing.

Anyone blessed to have been his student looked forward to his class-ending salutation, "I'll see you next time if 'The Creek' don't rise."

The news of his passing in February 2000 stunned me. A fund named the Thomas (Tom) Harold Folwell and Judith Oldham Folwell Scholarship was established in his name. In what was done with a touch of class, heartfelt love, and respect, Campbell named the beautiful fountain outside of the red brick Lundy-Fetterman School of Business, the Thomas H. Folwell Memorial Fountain, after its first dean of the business school. Folwell's inspiration influenced me to seek greater business knowledge, many years later, from Campbell's sister school, Mercer University

Once, while passing through "The Creek" on a seasonally cool but sunny early October afternoon, more than nine years after his death, I paused at the fountain in the Purvis Garden. The first thing I noticed was a quote engraved in stone, which affirmed that this was "a place for quiet reflection, indeed!"

I sat quietly on a crescent shaped concrete bench in the meditation area made possible by Ester Holder Howard, on the west side of the fountain. Like Folwell, who was energetic, the fountain shoots streams of aquatic energy into the air. The pool, which sits slightly elevated, southeast of the beautiful school of business, has one center spout with water leaping, almost thrusting upward, as if one could imagine, grasping for Heaven. It is surrounded by three smaller and lesser fountain ports positioned in symmetry, as if representative of the Trinity – Father, Son and Holy Ghost.

I get a sense that my brother Folwell is all right, that wherever he is, he is protected, and we will indeed see each other "…next time if 'The Creek' don't rise." May his memory and his warm agrarian spirit remain forever present, just as the fountain waters spout forth streams of energy near the school he loved so much.

Dr. Shelby Stephenson, English literature professor, and I would cross paths during my freshman year. He loved my writing style and I loved his class so much that I received an "A." Although the red-haired Stephenson's family origin appears to be English, he fit the ArgyllAmerica mold well because of his love for things simple, pure, old-fashioned, and rural. His life was the product of a resilient upbringing; he left his native Johnston County farm and his three-room plank board shanty near Benson, on "Paul's Hill," to better his education. He would later share the values learned on that farm as the youngest of four siblings, through the arts.

Thomas H. Folwell Memorial Fountain at Purvis Garden, Campbell University, NC

In a very subtle way, he was like my Henry Koch, founder of the Carolina Playmakers, and philosophy professor Horace Williams, both Paul Green's mentors while Green was a student at UNC-Chapel Hill. Even though I chose a different career path after graduation, he affects me still. In my dust-covered memory of that era, Stephenson, with his love of the American South and the rural settings depicted in music, poetry, and literature, looms with his booming voice.

I was not surprised that, in 2001, he received The North Carolina Award in Literature, the highest civilian award given by the Tar Heel State. Once the Chair of Campbell's English Department, he retired in 2010 as professor of literature and creative writing at the University of North Carolina – Pembroke; having served there since 1978 and editor of *Pembroke Magazine* since 1979.

Ernest R. Gilchrist

Campbell, during my college years, was a place where Music 131 was not just a class but an experience learned through life's lessons. It was a "fusion" of various tunes belting out from your dorm room, co-existing with the music of the guy next door or perhaps even your roommate's. It was where Peter Cetera and *Chicago* were enjoyed for their smooth melodies in tunes like "If You Leave Me Now" and "Baby What A Big Surprise," along with Rose Royce's smash hit "Carwash," and where a "Groove Line" was created by *Heat Wave*. The multicultural spirit of ArgyllAmerica embraced *Sugar Hill*'s marathon of a song, "Rapper's Delight." At on-campus events, *Mother's Finest* wanted to "Tell Me Something Good," the *Temptations* were reminding us about "My Girl," and Bill Deal and the *Rhondells* asked us "What Type of Fool Do You Think I Am?" as we danced to beach music, doing the shag.

Bumming a ride to Raleigh, the capital city, on Thursday nights to S-R-O while grooving to "I Love the Nightlife," and dancing the night away under the strobe lights in a capacity crowd to songs like "Fly Like An Eagle," "Ladies Night," "Flashlight," and "September" were simply "priceless." During these times I felt "We Are Family," as *Sister Sledge* did. Yes – S-R-O was usually Standing-Room-Only!

Sometimes, because of the stillness, the slow pace of "The Creek," it allowed me time to think and meditate, often on songs by artists like James Taylor. Many a day I half-hummed and half-sang part of the lyrics to "*Carolina In My Mind*":

"In my mind I'm goin' to Carolina
Can't you see the sunshine
Can't you just feel the moonshine
Maybe just like a friend of mine
It hit me from behind
Yes I'm goin' to Carolina in my mind…"

The University embraced U.I.A., Unity in Action, in which I was a participant. U.I.A. was like a Black Student Union, an opportunity for mostly African-American students on a majority white campus to seek fellowship together, do positive things like civic and community projects, and offer mutual support. We met every first and third Monday and Mr.

David Buckingham was our sponsor.

During my senior year, Campbell, having a rather large (comparatively speaking) and musically talented freshman minority class, birthed the Campbell Gospel Choir from U.I.A. We ministered to local churches in eastern North Carolina, praising God's name in song with hits like Andrae Crouch's "Take Me Back" and Tremaine Hawkins' "Going Up Yonder. "

A memorable but nervous moment was singing during Black History Month during Cultural Enrichment Program in 1980. This was different for Campbell, as many of the attendees were friends, classmates, and dorm mates, used to Southern gospel but not black gospel. It was great to share a part of our culture, as many had never witnessed a live black gospel performance before. It was also the beginning of progress, which set the table for more cultural reciprocity in years to come.

Campbell is a good ol' Baptist institution. The cartoon below from *Creek Pebbles* during the late seventies captures one of the things that I remember about campus life. Drinking was and still is against the rules. Among most students, it was one of those "don't ask, don't tell" things. The moral to the story is pretty straight-forward. Baptists are not perfect. Neither are Methodists, Catholics, Episcopalians, Muslims, or any denomination. They are people, too, subject to human frailties, and as I sometimes did, liked to unwind by having a drink or two. THOU SHALL NOT LIE.

Photo: Creek Pebbles Cartoon from the late 70s - Morning after the party

Ernest R. Gilchrist

CULTURAL ENRICHMENT PROGRAM

I WILL

I CAN

I AM

On many Tuesday and Thursday mornings in "The Creek," I attended C.E.P., the Cultural Enrichment Program. This was required for at least four semesters.

"Culture? Enrichment?" I would often ask - silently.

I sometimes felt, after leaving many of those programs, that it had been a form of forced culture. Each student had an assigned seat in Turner Auditorium of D. Rich Building. During the semester, a checker in the balcony verified his or her presence on the days that he or she was scheduled to attend. In all fairness to Campbell and its program administrator, it did appear to have a balance of programming during the semester. Nevertheless, I had to grow into the acceptance of that thought.

Then came another Thursday morning! It seemed that this day was different. I, along with many of my classmates, was alert – focusing on every word spoken! Perhaps it was also his articulation of the English language, accentuated by a thick Scottish accent, which rolled the syllables off his tongue like a drummer in a percussion section in staccato cadence. At least, that's the way it seemed from the beginning. I was suddenly transformed from being nonchalant, wanting the next 30 minutes to pass quickly, to a more energized and captive mature young man listening very intently to WISDOM. This man could relate! No, he did not appear to be youthful, for his gray hair was a dead giveaway. However, when C.E.P. adjourned, I, perhaps we, left more appreciative than when we arrived. Honestly, many years later, I don't remember anything else he said that day – and I'm sure it was awe-inspiring; just six words spoke to me. These were not mere words! They were words of motivation, of uplift, of progression. All I knew then was that if I were to succeed in life, including Campbell University and beyond, it could be found somewhere in those words.

I was so impressed by his mantra, his parting words, if you will, that I repeated it continuously in my head. On my return from classes to the dorm that day, I obtained a leftover cardboard box from Buies Creek Grocery and cut out a 5"x7" piece of cardboard. With a colored marker, I wrote the words, *I AM, I CAN and I WILL* in step progression from left to right.

My new mantra, *I AM, I CAN and I WILL,* was now etched in my mind and written on a brown rectangular fibrous board. It seemed to stare at me, and I at it, every time I sat at my desk in my dorm room in Murray Hall. No, I was not delusional, but just into these words. Perhaps, it was because it was something to support my adjustment to a campus that was only about 30 miles away from home but might as well have been 300 miles. I had no transportation, no "wheels," if you will. Therefore, I did not go off campus to visit very much. I knew that I was determined to make it – to succeed in Campbell's tough academic environment, as well as compete on the court.

The Latin, *Ad Astra Per Aspera* (To the Stars Through Difficulty) is Campbell's motto. I had to stick it out, for I was realizing my lifelong dream of being a scholarship student athlete.

Charles Reavis Adams used to call me "Ernie G from Benhaven." Benhaven High School, established in 1924 and located in the western Harnett County village of Olivia, meant "Hill of Refuge." I kind of liked that moniker and even adapted it as a way of identifying myself. Charles, a stand-out athlete from Angier, and I had been rivals in high school, competing in basketball.

Charlie Adams, Charles' father, served the North Carolina High School Athletic Association (NCHSAA) for more than 40 years, 25 of them as executive director. Charles and I forged a close friendship because of our former competitiveness on the hardwood, and he was very culturally at ease among blacks. We still enjoyed kidding each other. We'd spend hours talking about games we competed in and how he loved coming to "our house" because we warmed up in pre-games to the *Average White Band* and "That's the Way I Like It."

When I heard my appointed moniker, it reminded me of two things. First, it reminded me that I was a winner. Benhaven had a long-standing tradition of winning boys' and girls' high school basketball teams. It reminded me of my competitive nature.

Secondly, Charles' appointed moniker for me reminded me that my home in Harnett's Johnsonville Township, in the heart of the "sand barrens," was across the Cape Fear River. For me, the Cape Fear was a psychological dividing line in the County, in addition to an obvious natural one. West and southwest of the river was a land that seemed foreign to even many natives of the eastern and northern small towns and communities of Harnett. Author Malcolm Fowler, in his book *They Passed This Way,* said this of the Cape Fear River:

"In the mad days of the Revolution, Harnett, though it would not be a county for another 75 or more years, was a land divided, not only geographically but politically.

Physically, the Cape Fear River divided the area. On the east side of the river most of the people were Whigs-Patriots, if you please. This section had been settled largely by people from the eastern part of the state or by others coming down the old trail from Virginia, which went by the name of Green's path to the Pee Dee. It ran through eastern Harnett.

Not so on the western side. Save for the narrow strip along the river, settled by the Scots who came over prior to 1748, and a small area around Barbeque Church, the western side was settled by Scottish Highlanders with a thin sprinkling of other nationalities" (Fowler, They Passed This Way).

Maybe it was because of the more rural nature of western Harnett and surrounding communities that I seemed to have an edge. That is probably why these inspiring words of the Scotsman found me. There was a connection – a determination to succeed, despite my humble agrarian exposure to life.

When I finished Campbell in May 1980, I returned home to begin the transition to the next phase of my life. Packed among my things was a piece of sheet paper with my favorite mantra. The cardboard, replaced a few years before, now had a cleaner look.

Most people would have thrown away something, at first appearance, so seemingly unimportant. I remember placing my mantra sign on the dresser in the small bedroom my brother Herbert and I used to share, and continued unpacking. My thoughts would soon turn to things such as finding a job.

More than a year later, while visiting Herbert in his dorm room at East Carolina University, I noticed a familiar looking faded sign with what had become some very familiar words – *I AM, I CAN and I WILL.* Now, this was definitely a pleasantly surprising moment. Apparently, somewhere along the way, Herbert had adapted my mantra as his own.

Could he have seen my mantra sign in my dorm room upon frequent weekend visits to "The Creek"? Did he first adopt it in our bedroom, thinking that it was no longer any use to me? It really does not matter. What does matter is that he embraced the words *I AM, I CAN, and I WILL* as his own mantra. Perhaps that is what he used to help himself achieve the great success of becoming a highly recruited high school basketball player. While in the high school ranks, he accomplished or exceeded everything I had wanted to accomplish, athletically. As a graduating senior, Herbert was selected for the North Carolina East-West All-Star Basketball Game.

I am convinced that it was our mantra that became a driving psychological force, which led him to earn a basketball scholarship. Herbert would eventually play four years for the East Carolina University Pirates, graduate, marry, and raise three beautiful daughters.

Wow! The power of someone else's words or thoughts, shared with others, can have a life-changing effect on them.

THAT SPECIAL SEASON OF 1976-1977

It was the fall of 1984, November 10 to be exact, and another cool, crisp western New England morning had greeted us. Carlton Thompson, my former teammate, and I were in Springfield, Massachusetts, and the reality of what we had accomplished in 1977 really began to sink in.

I had been working on an industrial engineering waste-control management project in nearby Easthampton at the J.P. Stevens plant and had invited "T," who worked for Milliken, a competing, privately-held textile firm, up for a long weekend. He had never been to this part of the United States and neither had I, until about a year earlier, and I had planned to show him around.

"This is God's country," many locals would say, noting the beauty of the area. Natives also said the same thing about Patrick County, Virginia, which was where my job was based, in the foothills of the Blue Ridge Mountains.

A few months earlier, although I was still working for Stevens, my wife Synetha and I had moved from Collinsville, Virginia, to Decatur, Georgia – an eastern Atlanta suburb. When not in Virginia or Decatur, I mostly stayed in Holyoke, which is just north of Springfield, every other weekend.

"T," who was a groomsman in my wedding the year before, and I visited each other regularly. The last time we had met up was in the summer of 1984 for an exhibition game at the Greensboro Coliseum, featuring the U.S. Olympic Men's Basketball Team.

The "fellas," as we sometimes referred to ourselves, had planned a big-time outing, which included a Knicks vs. Bulls game at Madison Square Garden, a sightseeing tour of Manhattan, and later that weekend, a trip to the Basketball Hall of Fame.

I left Easthampton around noon on Thursday, via White Plains, en route to Newark International to pick up "P," who was flying in from Greensboro. Carlton had a few nicknames outside of "Eastwood," which was given to him by our mutual friend and Campbell schoolmate Lemuel Heckstall. "T" was a name that resonated with him, personally. You could tell that he really liked the latter and it may have preceded his coming to Buies Creek. However, "P" for "Partner" was interchangeable, and it applied to any teammate you paired up with in practice for shoot-around and other two or three-person drills.

After picking up "T" at Newark, we traveled to the Wyndham Hotel on Manhattan's Upper West Side, to 42 West 58th Street. Stevens had a corporate apartment there, and I had made a few phone calls and managed to reserve it for a couple of nights. Thanks to a previous visit to the city that fall with Jimmy Stowe, my wonderful boss at the time, and

Gordon Blackwell, the division's mechanical engineering director, and his wife, I was aware of the nice apartment.

We were so excited to be going to the storied "Garden" that we nearly didn't realize that 7th Avenue and West 33rd Street were two miles away. Besides, it was Michael's first game in this arena and the walking did not seem to bother us "country boys," as we were still in basketball playing shape. We were both frugal – too cheap to catch a taxi.

We were so proud of Jordan, a humble, hard-working, eastern North Carolina product, like us. Michael sharpened some of his basketball fundamentals as a camper at Campbell's Summer Basketball School, and it was there that he met our common friend and my teammate, Fred Whitfield, a counselor. MJ had exceeded nearly everyone's expectations from high school, coming out of Wilmington Laney, at that time not known for a history of being a basketball powerhouse, on to a memorable career at Carolina, and now in the pros.

I held my breath slightly as Michael gained his first possession of the ballgame.

"T," how can MJ miss that easy lay-up?" I asked loudly.

"T" replied, "He's just a little nervous…but wait, it's early. Besides, I've seen you miss a few lay-ups yourself back in 'The Creek,'" he recalled. "Shush!" "T" added, in a hushed voice.

MJ then proceeded to make five in a row.

"Awesome!" I shouted, ignoring Carlton's plea to let him concentrate.

MJ had made a steal off the Knicks as they attempted to inbound the ball on the Bulls' end of the court, dunked, and rocked the house.

"Homeboy!" Carlton exclaimed, coming out of his seat.

Next, Jordan drove baseline hard and made a signature double-pump, over-the-head, reverse dunk. We both rose out of our seats, slapping each other with high fives, as we gleamed with joy.

"MJ!" "T" yelled.

"Go Bulls!" I screamed.

I looked around, suddenly realizing, as we sat down, that we were surrounded by startled upset Knicks fans. "T" and I looked at each other and, without saying a word, turned our attention to the court, only to see Bernard King stop dead in his tracks, bewildered, as MJ fired another two points from the top of the key, in front of the Knicks superstar.

We were brave, especially considering that we were two Bulls fans in the Garden, carrying on as we did. We almost couldn't believe that we were having such great fun – especially Carlton, who patterned his hard work ethic after retired Bulls great Norm Van Lier, his favorite sports star. Nevertheless, we knew that we were not going to let anything or anyone stop us from having a good time. We were in the "Big Apple."

Later, Coach Kevin Loughery would pull Michael halfway through the fourth quarter to a rousing standing ovation from some very basketball-savvy New York fans.

"T" very confidently stated "it wasn't even close,"

The final score: Bulls 121, Knicks 106; MJ, 33 points.

We left the Garden assured that Jordan, whose Scotch-Irish surname, traceable to the roots of immigrants and the ancestors of former slaves in Wilmington and North Carolina's Coastal Plain, would someday end up where we were headed on Saturday – Springfield.

Saturday had finally come, and our long awaited trip to the campus of Springfield College and the Naismith Memorial Basketball Hall of Fame was upon us. We were aware that this location would close the following year to open near downtown Springfield on the east bank of the beautiful Connecticut River. That would be the second of what would be three locations for the Museum, since its existence.

Carlton and I were students of the game and had a lot of respect for the basketball history accumulated at the museum. "T" was a few paces in front of me when we entered the area for collegiate champions. As always, I liked to digest all the details.

Suddenly, I heard him say, "Look, 'P'! Just damn!"

Carlton had this look on his face, one that I had seen before.

"What!" I said, as I moved closer to see what was causing him to stare at the display so incredulously.

Under the area for NAIA Men's Champions for 1977 was Texas Southern University.

"No mention of number two, huh?" I asked dejectedly.

"No one cares about the runner-up! Yes. That would be us – Campbell College," Carlton responded.

I, like Carlton, stared at the inscription, reflecting on that memorable season in 1976-77…

We were very close. We were overcomers. We were resilient. Just like the farmers and the sharecroppers whom author and playwright Paul Green wrote about who lived in the North Carolina "sand barrens," eking out a meager existence, so were my teammates strong in our efforts to overcome an up, then down, then up again basketball season.

It was 1976 and Danny Roberts was my chain-smoking, tobacco-chewing coach of the Campbell College Men's Basketball team. It would be three more years before the Southern Baptist affiliated institution would reach university status. I will always be grateful to Coach Roberts because he gave this country boy an opportunity to live a dream nurtured from childhood.

Photo: 1976-77 NAIA Men's National Runnerups
Credit: Charles E. Bloodworth; Campbell University Archives

Roberts, a folksy but intense personality, recruited six freshmen, including me – three blacks and three whites, all North Carolina kids except one. They included Ben Lehman of Riverside, NJ; Darrell "Slick" Mauldin of New London's North Stanley High School; Jeff "Superbo" Newton from Beaufort's East Carteret High School; Keys Benston of Englehard and Mattamuskeet High School; Carlton, who was from Faison but attended Hobbton High School; and yours truly, "Ernie G," the southpaw from western Harnett County's Benhaven High School. Each of us had successful high school careers, respected each other's abilities, had excellent character, and were fierce competitors.

These young frosh joined forces with the upper classmen – four blacks and two whites – which included Sam Staggers, a native of Mullins, South Carolina; Kinston's Don Whaley; Donnie "Wiz" Laird of Sidney, New York; Clay Alston of Wake Forest; and Will Heckstall and John Heckstall, both from Colerain of Bertie County. Our team managers, Frank "Up" Upchurch of Fayetteville, North Carolina, and Howard "Howie" Britt of Clinton, North Carolina, were vital to our team's success both on and off the court.

My teammates and I worked diligently through the sweaty, humid August and September pre-season conditioning drills at little but quaint Carter Gym. I came to Buies Creek, a rural campus community, in basketball shape, having played and exercised all summer long. However, weightlifting was a major part of our conditioning drills at Campbell, as in most college programs, and it was new to me. I would later realize why I needed to get stronger, as college-level ball proved to be a more physical game than what I was accustomed to playing.

Sam Staggers was just a STUD! Only 6'6", Sam started at center, lean but strong as an ox. Staggers, from a small town just south of the North Carolina border, was fundamentally polished, sought perfection, "worked his ass off," and challenged each of us to be better. If a freshman sometimes made a stupid play in practice, Sam would practically get in his face to seize the opportunity to correct him. I experienced Staggers' wrath several times during the season. The positive thing about these "teaching moments" was that I could see excellence in him. I also knew the personal side of Sam, as I shared a dorm suite with him. That side of Sam was always friendly, fun loving, and welcoming.

Don Whaley, one of best athletes on the squad, was a world-class softball player, as well. Whaley was quick, could "jump out of the gym," and had a difficult jumper to defend, as he had a slight fade away. At 6'3", Whaley was just as comfortable as a big guard or small forward. One of his most important attributes was his wit and humor. He had a great sense of humor and it was fun to be in his presence. Like his fellow seniors on the team, Whaley, as playful as he often was, held his teammates accountable on the court.

Donnie "Wiz" Laird was meek, humble, and very respectful off the court. However, it would have been a mistake if a competitor mistook that for weakness. Donnie, the starting point guard, was tough and was one of the team's better defenders! You did not see him too often on campus without Jenny, whom he would later marry, shortly after graduation. It did not take long after I had set foot on campus for me to realize he was smart. I would notice Staggers in "Wiz" first floor suite on the other end of Murray Hall – witha book. "Wiz" was very generous of his time.

Clay Alston, a former outstanding high school quarterback at Wake Forest-Rolesville, near Raleigh, was a physically strong, fundamentally sound, savvy basketball player at shooting guard. I sometimes paired off with Clay, a JUCO from Brevard College, in practice drills and often defended him in scrimmages. His natural strength and experience was often too much for my physical abilities, especially towards the end of those grueling practices.

Off the court, Clay wore glasses, which when he dropped them down over his nose to see up close, gave him the appearance of a professor. Alston, a former all-Metro performer in high school, had a competitive but humble spirit and complemented Laird well in the backcourt.

Will and John were the "salt of the earth." Blood brothers and often referred to jointly as simply "the Heckstalls," they were probably two of the most athletic players on the team. Will, at 6'5", was also a trackster, and built with a NFL type body. Gifted athletically, he ran the lanes extremely well and fast. John, at 6'6", was not quite as athletic as his brother, as he was more slender but very fundamentally sound.

According to Coach Roberts, John had a high basketball IQ, saying that John was one of the smartest basketball players he had coached.

I liked the Heckstalls because they came from Bertie County and Colerain, a small town with an agrarian culture in the northeastern part of North Carolina's Coastal Plain. We sometimes had our differences… always small. Both brothers were outspoken and sometimes I thought their opinions desired more tactfulness. Nevertheless, they were often right. For example, the team exchanged gag gifts for Christmas in 1976. Will pulled my name and gave me a brown plastic basketball yoyo. It was the "Fred Flintstone Yabba Dabba Doo!" type. His point was that by being a natural lefty, I was not skilled enough dribbling hard to my right – especially under pressure.

"Gil' can't go right!" Will would yell, often telling me that I needed to work on getting better.

Although Will was on point, it took a lot initially for me to accept the truth about a weakness. Yeah, it stung a little bit when I opened up the gift in front of my teammates. I played the embarrassment off with a shrug and a laugh. My teammates knew it was true, too, but they admired me for my obvious strengths such as quickness, passing, defending, and overall camaraderie.

Ben Lehman was the oldest freshman among us, as he was our senior by several years. He was extremely hardworking, perhaps over-compensating for what might have been perceived as a lack of athletic ability. However, he was one of the most fundamentally sound players, apparently influenced by older brothers George and Austin Lehman. George, a former ABA star, was a "professional shooting instructor." He conducted clinics focused on the "Art of Shooting," utilizing the four basic steps of shooting – balance, eye on the target, elbow straight, and follow-through. During his clinics, George used the Pro-Keds® Toss®Back, a basketball fundamental training device with which Ben displayed an above average level of expertise.

Ben was one of only two players from "up north" and sometimes was perceived as brash and very direct. That was just the "Jerzey" in him. Beneath it was a very warm and genuine spirit. You could tell he cared for people. I remember having conversations off the court with "Bennie," and he revealed to me a man of real character and feelings – somewhat different from his almost robotic on the court basketball playing style.

Darrell Mauldin had one of the smoothest jump shots of any teammate, honed, no doubt, from countless hours in the gym. I mean, it was really "sweet!" Well-mannered and well-groomed, Darrell fit the nickname "Slick" very well. Legend has it that Mauldin did not leave his dorm room in Kitchin Hall to walk across campus unless everything was just right, especially the hair. But the most impressive thing about Darrell was not the hair that he always kept in place, the iron-pressed creases in his clothes, or his fundamentally "flawless" jump shot. No, impressive were his impeccable manners and a humble, meek spirit – evidence of what I perceived as being the product of a strong Christian home. Darrell, in his sophomore year, became the NCAA Division I Free Throw Percentage Champion, meeting the minimum number required for qualification.

"John Jefferson 'Superbo' Newton," I often said, calling him by his full name. Jeff earned his team appointed nickname 'Superbo' honestly, sometimes using his sharp elbows in an attempt to gain a superior advantage on the court, especially against taller players. Most of the time, it wasn't necessary, as he was one of the hardest working and fundamentally sound players on the team. Like Carlton, he was often a pairing up partner, a "P" in practices. Understandably, it was not uncommon to hear him refer to others, especially Carlton or me, as "P".

Jeff, an academic scholar and a member of Phi Kappa Phi, grew up down east near the Atlantic Coast and was perhaps my most cultured and well-traveled teammate. His parents were well educated and supportive of his career. His father was a renowned oceanographer. John G. Newton led the expedition that discovered the sunken Civil War ironclad, the *Monitor*. The famous battle runner was found 16 nautical miles off the coast of Cape Hatteras, three years before Jeff entered Campbell as a freshman. Mr. and Mrs. John G. Newton and Jeff's younger brother Rhett often made the three-hour drive from the historic seaport of "Beaufort Town" to "The Creek," The 6'6" Rhett would join his brother the next year, becoming a future teammate. I marveled at Jeff's having that type of support, as my parents, who loved me dearly, never attended games at home and had slightly more than a 30-minute ride across the county. Ironically, my parents were not really into basketball.

Coach Roberts said that Jeff had "great parents."

Newton showed great enthusiasm on the "hardwood" and was an excellent teammate, blending well with all personalities. I learned a lot from the lanky Newton, a former star track and field high jumper. Today, I eat the entire baked potato, skin and all, because of his influence. Sure, I grew up planting and digging up potatoes in the family garden, but I did not know that eating the potato skin was healthy because of all the nutrients. If I'm not mistaken, I learned some tips on cutlery, too.

Keys Benston, like our teammate Jeff, was from down east near the Atlantic Ocean, as well. He grew up in one of the most beautiful areas of the state, in Hyde County, near Lake Mattamuskeet, the largest lake in North Carolina, and the Pamlico Sound. Benston spoke with a very pronounced, almost Elizabethan English accent with the "o" sound being very long. Words like coach, boat, and house sounded like "coech, boet, and haowse." We loved his accent. Keys, an excellent student, very hard worker, and gentle giant at 6'8", brought a unique cultural balance to the team. Along with Sam and Will, Keys was perhaps one of the strongest players on the squad. He had what appeared to be a lot of latent strength.

Carlton was my best friend on the team. Wherever you saw him, you often saw me. Periodically, some students would ask if we were brothers. To such inquiries, we would respond, "No way!" Like fellow teammate Clay Alston, he was a high school quarterback at his Newton Grove alma mater, located about an hour east of "The Creek." "T" had talent and lots of athleticism, but while just above 6'1" was forced to play out of position at small forward. Like me, an athlete who grew up attending a rural school, his ball handling was not refined enough to earn desirable minutes playing guard in the college game. His shooting was great, especially with his high leaping vertical, as he could fire the "living daylights" out of the basketball. That is how he earned the additional nickname "Eastwood," as in Hollywood's gun-slinging actor whose first name is Clint. Ironically, Clint Eastwood was also his favorite film star, along with Pam Grier.

Carlton was a very good student, had the highest of character, and it seemed that everyone liked him. We had a lot in common off the court and later in our academic careers would become business majors. I knew that "T" was my true friend because he kidded me hard and, as necessary, vented his frustrations, and I likewise. I reciprocated by often allowing myself to be the butt of his good-hearted jokes and by listening with my heart, as well as my ears.

If anyone has ever met me, they would know that I am not 6'1". That was my listed program height…that I provided. I am barely 6'0", more 5'11¾". Coach Roberts and most of my teammates overlooked my "fantasy." Chances are that they discounted it as an inflated ego from a country kid who sometimes struggled internally to prove that he deserved to be there like everyone else, people from bigger places. Carlton was probably the only teammate that "called me out" on it. "T" had a way of being painfully honest with me.

I continued the trend of being a local Harnett County product on a Danny Roberts team. He had coached others before me, like Wayne Sanford and Bob Wells from the nearby towns of Coats and Angier, respectively. It was something I quietly embraced with a lot of pride. No, this sole representation did not mean that I was the best. Honestly, I felt that there were more gifted, talented, and athletic players who had come before me at my alma mater, Class 1-A Benhaven, and could have easily played at Campbell. I had enough talent, athleticism, and smarts to get the attention of Roberts, resulting in an opportunity to play on the college level. I was well-rounded and would be considered a complementary player.

An opportunity to play in a Campbell College Summer Basketball School pickup game with a cast of other more talented players solidified attaining my scholarship. In June 1976, my high school coach and friend Fred Davis arranged an opportunity for me to travel across the county to "The Creek" one evening to play a few games with the college and professional basketball counselors in Carter Gym. Davis, a Roanoke Rapids native, had played basketball at northeastern North Carolina's Chowan College before transferring to Campbell. However, he did not play for Coach Fred McCall in the late 1960s, as he focused on academics and starred in intramurals, which according to Davis were very competitive.

Gerald Henderson, Sr. of Virginia Commonwealth University, Marc Iavaronni, a 6'8"forward from the University of Virginia, and a few others were my teammates. Both Henderson and Iavaronni would go on to play professional ball. Gerald, a lanky, smooth, 6'2' shooting guard from Richmond, would play for numerous NBA teams but is most famous for his heroics as a Boston Celtic, when in game two of the 1984 NBA Championship he stole James Worthy's in-bound pass. This fascinating play enabled his team to win the game in overtime. Marc, a native New Yorker, would make his mark with the 76ers and start as a mature 26-year old "rookie" on the 1983 NBA Championship team.

We played against M.L. Carr, a 6'6" hard-nosed defensive stopper, who played for numerous NBA squads. The rugged Carr, a Guilford College graduate, later would both play and coach for the Boston Celtics. Mark Crow of Duke, the sleek and silky Clyde "The Glide" Austin, a high school All-American out of Richmond's Maggie Walker High School, and a couple of others rounded out the opponents. I held Clyde, a future member of the N.C. State Wolfpack, in check, stripping him of the ball on one trip down court, made a few baskets and the rest is history. Of course, it didn't hurt having Gerald and Marc as teammates. Guys, I owe you both big-time for unknowingly helping, through our impressive play, to convince Coach Roberts to offer me a full scholarship!

Unfortunately, Clay only played his junior year (my freshman year) for the Fighting Camels due to academic difficulties. I shared a suite with both Sam and Clay in Murray Hall and got to know them well, although as a "newbie" I kept my door closed a lot. Clay stayed right across the hall with his roommate McChell Jackson, who was from Virginia. "Chelly" was the one I had to stay clear of on a social basis if I wanted to stay focused. Staggers stayed diagonally across the hall beside Clay, and Mike Evans, a baseball player, was his roommate. I remember Mike as being one of the nicest people anyone would want to meet. James "Wiley" McLean's room was adjacent to mine. James was a three-year starter and former North Carolina All-State shooting guard from Lumberton. He and I were opposites but our personalities were attracted to each other. Unfortunately, due to personal problems, he received a one-year suspension from the team before pre-season started.

Gone now were four starters from the previous season's 23-4 team, along with 60.5 points per game. This situation caused Coach Roberts to say, "Really, if we can go .500 in our first 10 games, I'll be pleased." Leading the group of former players was 1976 NAIA Third Team All-American guard Marshall Lovett.

Not expected to overwhelm anyone this season, the Fighting Camels won 13 of the first 16 games. This was a pleasant surprise. During this time, we had two major winning streaks – the first five games and then six straight, starting at game 11 with Belmont Abbey.

We endured a lot during the course of the regular season. Things began to get tenser at one of our away games because of the impact of Alex Haley's *Roots*, the epic miniseries. Racial tensions were affecting, for better or worse, the raw emotions of some people. This was evident at our February 16 game with Fayetteville State University at the Cumberland County Memorial Arena. They were the first Historical Black College & University (HBCU) that we had on the schedule since the mini-series electrified the country.

The Broncos, beaten by fifteen points at the hands of the Camels on the same floor in early December, were red hot. Even though this game was played away from Fayetteville State's home gym, their fans traveled the few miles across town to support them on this school night. They were very intense and vocal, standing at their seats behind us, keeping the required distance.

Roots had mesmerized the American TV audience since its initial airing in late January. "Kunta Gilchrist, Kunta Thompson, Toby Benston" said some creative fans stationed behind our bench, referencing our last names affixed to the back of our orange and black uniforms. They were intent to rub the lopsided loss into our players' psyche. Immersed so (as we all had been) into Kunta Kinte's culture and journey from West Africa, they even called Coach Roberts "Massa" for slave master. This was one of those games that you couldn't wait to finish – counting down the final minutes and seconds. The 40 minutes of misery now finally over, we sprinted to the northwest end of the building towards the locker room, dodging celebratory fans, and embarrassed by our 24-point loss still reflected on the scoreboard.

One Bronco cheerleader was so caught up in the "*Roots, Kunta Kinte, Toby, Massa*" thing that she nearly spit on me – just missing my face. I ducked and quickly looked at her in astonishment, continuing to pass. I struggled internally with what had happened for several days.

"Why would someone be so confused and anguished because of watching the riveting TV drama, (a depiction of history that cannot be changed), that they would look to express it by doing something so humanly demeaning?" I pondered.

It did not matter that I was black like she was. What she saw was my uniform, which represented a predominately-white institution. I eventually let it go, asking God to forgive her. I knew that the legacy of Fayetteville State, founded by the "visionary seven," was above any over-emotional response to a ballgame. Many of my relatives – people I felt good about…that I loved - graduated from the university off Murchison Road.

Going into Methodist College, we were pathetic, having lost five of the previous eight games, including back-to-back home losses to Elon and Guilford the previous week. If not for an away victory on Valentine's Day in Myrtle Beach against Coastal Carolina, we might have lost all confidence.

As I left my dorm room for Carter Gym to catch the bus on Saturday, February 19, Manfred Mann's *Earth Band*'s number one Billboard hit, a version of Bruce Springsteen's song "Blinded by the Light," was playing in my head. Recently, it had been heating up the airwaves of local radio stations, often pumping the psychedelic sounds via blaring speakers down into the courtyard between Sauls and Murray Residence Halls.

It began to drizzle as we left Buies Creek, headed to Methodist, located on Fayetteville's Ramsey Street. The temperature felt decent, though, having warmed up a little, snapping the cold spell of the previous two days.

The lowest point of the season was arguably the loss to Methodist. Campbell's men had defeated the Monarchs 10 of the previous 11 games during the decade of the 1970s. This would be only the second loss in the 15-year history of the series – the first loss ever at Methodist.

Perry Jenifer, the *Fayetteville Times* Sports Editor, described the scene in the visitors' locker room after the game as well as any Hollywood scriptwriter could. In his Sunday morning column titled, "Where It Began, Grasping for Straws, Where It Ended," he described the very solemn, subdued manner in which we quietly showered, dressed, and left the room. The pain was too great to make eye contact or to speak with our worn, emotionally distraught coach, who sat on a bench, nervously lighting up cigarette after cigarette.

... "Good kids," Danny Roberts sighed.

"Good kids," he said again. They make their grades, no problems there. They work hard, give you no trouble.

"And ... nice. So nice."

He started at the sound of that four-letter word. Like a man who just cut himself shaving.

"Maybe that's it," he said, stomping a smoked out cigarette beneath his shoe and reaching inside his suit coat for a fresh one. "Maybe we're too nice. We're too nice and need a couple of nasty kids."

... "When things start going bad, it's like when they are going good. I guess," said Roberts, a man whose style is not guess-work but who admittedly had been reduced to grasping at straws

by the turn of events which threatened to lay waste to a season filled with such promise.

The notion that his players were "too nice" was another straw.

"I've never seen you quite like this," a listener remarked. "Not in what...three, four years? You've lost before. "

Roberts nodded.

"I've never been down like this before," he agreed. "We're getting beat by teams that have no business beating us...if we play. We're not playing, not with any enthusiasm. We have no patience. We stand around like we've got magnets on our feet. We don't go after loose balls, rebounds." (Perry Jenifer, Fayetteville Times)

That night, little did we know that the stinging defeat, 61 to 57, would be the antihistamine needed to jumpstart what was an underachieving ball club. What seemed to have been the longest trip ever of only 30 miles up I-95 and west on U.S. Highway 421, through a thunderstorm and rain, to the sleepy little campus near the Cape Fear River, was arguably the season's turning point. We were "blinded by the light" of the Monarchs, but simultaneously it allowed us to increase our basketball senses as we went forward.

It was a cool Wednesday evening on March 2, 1977, in Four Oaks, North Carolina, at South Johnston High School, site of the NAIA District 29 Men's Basketball Championships. The temperature had been hovering around the mid-forties that day, even though it had been close to freezing earlier that morning. David Soul's song "Don't Give Up on Us Baby" (Tony Macauly) was burning up the charts in the UK and was beginning to get some radio playing time in the States. Even though it was a "breakup song," some of the lyrics seemed appropriate to describe my team's journey thus far, in a non-romantic sense, its inner struggle, and the relationship with our fans.

"Don't give up on us, baby
We're still worth one more try

I know we put our last one by
Just for a rainy evening
When maybe stars are few
Don't give up on us, I know we can still come through"

The NAIA District 29 Championship featured Elizabeth City State University (ECSU), winners of the Northern Division over Hampton-Sydney, and the Camels, who had defeated Pembroke State University in a closely contested battle, to settle the Southern Division. Established in 1887 as the State Normal School for Indians, Pembroke State had a very important history in North Carolina education. We were fortunate to defeat the Braves for the second time during the season.

It was a weird game, one that saw ECSU Coach Bobby Vaughn pull his players off the court with 2:02 remaining, claiming "this game is rigged." The coolness in the night air outside could not control the hysterics caused by their refusal to play, which gave the referees no choice but to call the game with the score 89-75, advancing us forward to Kansas City. The sweet taste of victory felt at that moment easily erased the unusual game-ending way we achieved it.

"Little Campbell College," as some sports analysts would soon refer to us, had received a tremendous boost of confidence.

Still, nothing in our wildest imaginations had prepared us for the euphoric, almost fantasy-like journey we would soon make.

Our team trip to the NAIA Championships was fascinating. This was Coach Roberts' second trip, having taken a talented team to the tourney in 1970, only to lose to Jackson State by two points. It revealed many firsts. I had never been to Missouri, let alone Kansas City. Unlike Jeff, Carlton, a few others, and I had never flown on an airplane. Sure, growing up in the shadow of Pope Air Force Base, I had seen my share of military aircraft flying in the skies above, but never had I flown in one. Jeff's calm, jovial nature steadied us as we boarded our Eastern Airlines flight at Raleigh-Durham Airport that included a planned changeover in Atlanta and stopover in St. Louis, Missouri.

That one extraordinary week spent in KCMO was definitely a "show me" experience. We saved our best basketball for the final week of the season. With Campbell upperclassman Dan Hart, our number one fan and unofficial cheerleader leading the way, we charged through the tournament like a midwestern tornado. The NAIA tourney committee did not seed us in this 32-team event.

Thank God, our first game was Monday evening's last contest, a 10:45 p.m. CST start! I spent practically all day Sunday and Monday tracking down my gym bag. My uniforms and game shoes were packed in my gym bag. No gym bag…no uniform…no dressing out. It was that simple.

Finally, my gym bag had been rushed back to Kansas City, but it would first travel errantly to Pittsburgh and West Germany before arriving at Kemper Arena fifteen minutes before game time. Whew! I released some nervousness and angst of anxiety. Somewhere along the way, perhaps in Atlanta, my gym bag did not change planes with the team's luggage and equipment. I could tell by my teammates' expressions that they had been feeling sorry for me, as it appeared that I might miss a momentous opportunity. We then went on to defeat Lincoln Memorial of Tennessee, seeded sixth, 76-75. Metaphorically, the shockwaves began within the arena moments after the final buzzer, as reporters and the basketball world's disbelief shook the nearby stockyards and sent a ripple effect into the waters at the confluence of the Missouri River and the Kansas River.

The day after Lincoln Memorial, we had a break in our schedule before playing Southwestern Oklahoma State. The team unwound by going to the movies to see *A Star Is Born*, featuring Barbara Streisand and Kris Kristofferson. Our star was definitely rising, as we were no longer a secret. We were riding high. Back home in "The Creek" they were going nuts.

"We were never in it," summed up Southwestern Coach George Hauser, referring to the lunch-hour basketball game. "They outplayed us from the start," Hauser stated, describing his team's 71-56 defeat at the hands of the Camels.

We humbled the Bulldogs with our defensive prowess as our opponent had averaged 86 points per game leading into the March 9 game.

Interestingly enough, for the next three games after Lincoln Memorial, we did not just win, we "spanked" our opponents – something not even we thought was possible.

There were several future NBA draft choices that season to play in the NAIA Tourney but not as our opponents. Most notable was the wiry floppy blonde center, Jack Sikma, of Illinois Wesleyan, who was one of the bigger stars representing his school. Sikma, who possessed a deadly pivoting jump shop, later that year got drafted eighth overall by the Seattle Supersonics. Although Sikma was an outstanding collegian (NAIA All-American), the Titans did not get past the quarterfinals, eventually losing to Henderson State 87-73.

Described as a team of the future, an athletic, tall Alcorn State University started three freshmen and two sophomores. One freshman, Larry Smith, was a tremendous force for the Braves, along with teammates Alfredo Monroe and Clinton Wyatt. Smith, who became a future Golden State Warrior, was drafted in the NBA's second round in 1980. He fought valiantly for his team before fouling out in their collision with the Camels in the quarterfinals, only to lose 77-63.

Our tenacious "bumble bee defense" (Braves had 24 turnovers) and team effort caused Coach Roberts to say, "Whaley ran it," referring to his flawless execution of the four corners. Due to Wiz's foul trouble and eye injury, Whaley stepped in big, working magic in an offense Dean Smith had made famous.

> *"Campbell College's amazing Camels continued to be the Cinderella team of the National NAIA Tournament here Thursday…"*
>
> *"Tobacco and basketball," Campbell College Coach Danny Roberts gushed after his team's 77-63 upset victory Thursday night over 4th-seeded Alcorn State in the quarterfinal round of the NAIA post-season tournament. "That's what our area is known for. And as far as I'm concerned basketball is number one." (UPI, The Fayetteville Observer.")*
>
> *"I don't know how we keep doing it," said Whaley, shaking his head and smiling. "But I just hope we don't run out of gas now."*
>
> *After the game, Coach Roberts confessed, "I never expected to be here this season." He continued, telling A.J. Carr, a*

Raleigh News and Observer staff writer, "*We've had much more talented teams the last three years that lost in the District finals. But this team has character and is gutsy.*"

"*It has worked hard and simply come out here and got its game together. They've done everything they've supposed to have done. Our bubble might burst tomorrow, but right now it's an inflated bubble,*" *Roberts said proudly.*

Second-seeded Illinois Wesleyan, led by Sikma, was upset by seventh-seeded Henderson State in the quarterfinals. The Reddies were runner-ups in the previous year's championship, having lost to Coppin State. The Arkadelphia, Arkansas-based school had an impressive record and came into the semifinal game at 29-3.

The Reddie Spirit and all of Henderson's resilient school history, like staying together despite the odds (fire once severely damaged campus), could not overcome having played the 10:30 p.m. game three straight nights, starting Tuesday. It finally took a toll on them. Led by Staggers with 29 points, we dismantled Henderson in a televised game before a friendly crowd of 6,156, by a score of 76 to 52. Our opponents didn't get into double figures until midway near the first half. Not able to catch up, unable to penetrate the Camel defense or hit from the outside, the game was virtually over at half time, as we commanded a 21-point lead.

"*We played very, very good,*" *Roberts said.* "*We did what we wanted to defensively. I think that showed when we held them to 19 points in the first half. We didn't want to get rubbed off and let them get the easy basket.*"

"*They played tremendous basketball,*" *said Don Dyer, the Henderson coach.* "*It was the worst beating we've taken in years. They shot so well in the first half. We didn't react. They hurt us in every way there is.*"

"*Staggers played great.,*" *said Roberts.* "*But everybody just played great.*"*(Cathie Burnes, The Kansas City Times)*

Gentle showers fell over Kansas City because of a major winter snowstorm in northwest Kansas. The sudden chill in the air over the last couple of days, ranging from the upper 30s to the lower 50s, along with the cold rain, created a cloud cover over Kansas City quite contrasting with the bright sunshine earlier in the week. The locals welcomed the rain that fell over Kemper Arena and vicinity. However, it was not enough to negate the drought that had set in since the previous mid-September.

Texas Southern stood in the way of our Cinderella-on-testosterone-like season. The Tigers, from the Southwestern Athletic Conference (SWAC), had lost in the NAIA Tourney quarterfinals to Coppin State the year before. Their drought of one year ago would not keep them from being in the winner's circle this time around.

It seemed that nothing we had done to other teams during the week would work on them. They were just better – too big, too strong, too talented. It would have required a near-flawless performance from us to beat them. In the first four games, we were able to contain our opponents' sharpshooters due to our changing defenses, controlling tempo and not seeing much zone defense, especially not a tightly packed 1-3-1 zone. The Tigers had solved the mysterious puzzle which had allowed Campbell's journey to *Alice in Wonderland* possible. They had been able to do what no one else had done in our victories during regular and postseason play.

In the second half, while sitting on the "pine," long after the outcome had been decided, I, along with a few of my teammates, took notice of the Texas Southern cheerleaders. Those lovely young ladies, in their maroon and gray, were "fine as wine" and were electrifying to watch as they stomped, clapped, and stepped. Our momentary distraction from the game in the final minutes spoke volumes about our broken-heartedness with the outcome.

This HBCU, located in Houston, Texas, would no longer be denied. Led by two future NBA draft choices, tourney most valuable player Alonzo Bradley and the sharp-shooting Lawrence Williams, they spanked our "assess" 71 to 44. It was the largest margin of defeat for any team in a championship game in tournament history. Bradley was drafted by the Indiana Pacers in Round 2 (7th pick, 29th overall). He never played for the Pacers as he was traded to the Houston Rockets, eventually playing three seasons. Williams was the 75th player chosen, (Round 4, 9th pick) by the

Kansas City Kings but was cut and would never don their uniform.

"This is not how the story was supposed to end," I thought, grimacing, trying to be strong as the game ended.

"We figured it up and I think we were 23-0 this year against teams that played us man-to-man," said Coach Roberts, reflecting on the finals en route home early Sunday morning. "Against teams that zoned us we were 0-10. The zone thing seemed to become a psychological matter."

"They've just got a great club," said Danny Roberts, realizing his team had simply run into a human howitzer. "They hit about their first 10 shots and we were out of it. We could never get into our game.

On defense, we just weren't skilled enough to stop them. They were good, tough."

"They were big and they closed it off inside," lamented Roberts, whose team shot 37.9 percent for the game. "We've got good shooters but the shots just weren't falling."

"They played zone and nobody else had played one against us," said Sam, who sat slump-shouldered on the Campbell bench at game's end. "It's good to have come this far...but heck, we should have won this tournament.." (A.J. Carr, The News and Observer)

Sam made NAIA All-tournament first team and Whaley made second team. 'Wiz' earned the Charlie Stevenson Hustle Award, his tenacity that his teammates had seen all season long rewarded. It was no surprise that our team won the sportsmanship trophy. That just summed up the respect that we had gained during the course of the week. What a fitting honor. In the end, though bittersweet, the Fighting Camels had made history, becoming the only unseeded team in the 40-year history of the NAIA National Tournament to play in the championship game.

The locker room was somber with quite a few restrained tears – no crying though.

"I wanted to win this one for the seniors on the team,"
said Clay Alston, his eyes misty, his voice haltering. "I'll be back
here." (A.J. Carr, The News and Observer)

But after the tears had dried and gone away, thoughts turned to celebration of our successful season. "Party, party, party" were the thoughts of many teammates, including me.

"Listen up guys," Coach Roberts said, as we finished getting dressed. "We've got to fly back tonight!"

"Ah, man!" could barely be heard from a few in the room, disappointed that a proper celebration worthy of our significant achievement would be delayed. However, our love and respect for Coach Roberts was greater than the thrill of bar hopping in downtown Kansas City. After leaving what had become our temporary residence for nearly a week, the historic Radisson-Meuhlebach Hotel, we departed on a chartered 1:45 a.m. flight.

Having stopped over in Chicago and Atlanta, we prepared for a 7:45 a.m. landing into the quiet Carolina morn', still somewhat stunned from our not so heroic finish back in KCMO just hours before, and weary from the quicker than expected transition. As we exited the plane at Raleigh-Durham Airport, the school pep band and approximately 100 cheering fans and students were there to greet us. It was a surreal setting, which helped to reinforce the bigness or the scale of being NAIA National Runner-ups. A "Way To Go Campbell" banner, written in bright orange letters, helped give the appearance of a campus pep rally.

Our reception at the airport provided a boost of energy. We excitedly boarded the bus to make the one hour journey southeast to the "The Creek," through the long leaf pines on the edge of the Sandhills.

Students were going bonkers as the bus pulled up on the street in front of Marshbanks! Toilet paper streamed from the trees in the campus green between the cafeteria and the science building. This was a shared experience, a rollercoaster ride like no one had ever witnessed in school history.

Photo: Coach Danny Roberts & Sam Staggers
Credit: Charles E. Bloodworth; Campbell University Archives

"It was fantastic here last week," one student said. The excitement was greater here every day. Everyone was walking around campus smiling all the time.

"You knew what was on everyone's mind. Every time we won there were cheering and yelling here that could be heard for a couple of miles." (UPI, The Fayetteville Observer)

"This is an emotional moment for all of us because there just aren't enough words to describe the way we feel" said Roberts, donned in a somewhat wrinkled leisure suit.

"It was just a beautiful week and even though we lost in the finals, it was a thrill just to be there playing for the national championship. The people in Kansas City just got turned on by our kids. But we were representing the folks back here in Buies Creek. It's great to be back home." (Perry Jenifer, Fayetteville Times)

"This team hasn't had as much talent as the other teams I've played on," said senior Sam Staggers, a first-team All-Tournament selection. "But it has more unity. There's no dissension. Everybody had great confidence in each other.

"Nobody thought we could win out here – but us." (A.J. Carr, The News and Observer)

"When you realize that there are hundreds of schools in the NAIA, it makes it even more unbelievable what this team did," Dr. Wiggins told the banquet audience. "I know that this sounds trite but I had people stopping me on the sidewalks telling me how much they liked our team-not just for their play but how they acted.". (Perry Jenifer, Fayetteville Times)

"Wiggins told the group "this is the best Sunday school class I've attended in a long time." Campbell is a Baptist supported college." (UPI, The Fayetteville Observer).

"You know there were a lot of cocky teams out there who didn't really look like they appreciated even playing in the tournament," said Whaley, while sipping punch.

"Maybe that's why the security people in the Kemper Arena liked us. We looked like regular people and defied the odds every night when we won. Nobody can take this past week from us. We may never enjoy anything like this again in our life-but we

can cling to this. It's really hard to put all this in words." (Perry Jenifer, Fayetteville Times)

Staggers' individual contribution, which undoubtedly, with the contribution of others, led to our team's success, was rewarded by being named NAIA First-Team All-American. According to Fighting Camels statistics, Sam set a Campbell career high, with 1957 points, eclipsing the former scoring record held by Johnny Marshbanks by 234. When this magic ride ended, Sam finished as the leading rebounder in school history, too. He would later go undrafted by the NBA but played European professional basketball in Belgium.

My NAIA National Runner-up team embodied the essence of ArgyllAmerica. It had racial harmony, resiliency, and sustainability. No, not sustainability in the natural or environmental sense, but from the perspective of being able to endure the highs and lows of what was an incredible season in Campbell sports history.

Carlton and I suddenly broke our focus at the display for what was a few seconds but what seemed to be an eternity on our missed opportunity for Campbell's entry into the Naismith Basketball Hall of Fame. We both shrugged it off and, as we did the day post-Texas Southern, 'moved on' to the next display.

Our mutual friend and Campbell schoolmate Debra Dunston delivered the unexpected news of Carlton's death one Monday on September 23, 2002, a morning that had started out like any other.

"Ernie," Debra said, obviously sobbing and trying to compose herself. "Carlton's gone!"

There was numbing silence on my end for a moment as I in what seemed like sonic speed reflected on my last visit with him a month prior. I thought about how healthy he looked and how happy I was leaving Rock Hill, South Carolina, where he lived, thinking that our friendship was back on track after spending several years being out of touch. Oh! The pain of those sorrowful words caused my heart to throb incredibly. You never expect death to come so soon for someone so young, fit and full of life. A hollow pit formed in my stomach and my senses dulled as I thought of what might have been his last moments. With tears streaming down my face, I thought of his family back in Faison and other places, and the tremendous hurt and shock that they must have been experiencing.

Four days later, we gathered at Carlton's home church, Holly Grove Church of Christ, Disciples of Christ, in rural Sampson County, outside of Clinton, North Carolina, for his home going. Many people from our Campbell family came to pay respects to "T". Among the mourners supporting his family were Charles Adams, Debra Dunston, Jeff Newton, Coach Roberts and Fred Whitfield. Fred, a transfer my sophomore year from UNC-Greensboro, befriended Carlton as well and was a fellow business major. Carlton's basketball career at Campbell was short-lived, lettering only one year, but he had a magnanimous spirit, which touched the lives of many people.

I was one of many pallbearers; most being Carlton's high school classmates or teammates. It seemed awkward sitting there in the little country church's 'Amen Corner,' somberly engaged in the gut-wrenching reality of the funeral service. He left us suddenly…much too soon at age 44 – all of us wanting to have another conversation, a hearty laugh, a game of HORSE, a round of golf, that could never be again. If "T" could talk today, he'd say that "44 is a good number – Hank Aaron, Jerry West, Reggie Jackson, "Pistol" Pete Maravich, Jim Brown, George "Iceman" Gervin, Elvin Hayes and Franco Harris wore 44." He loved sports and had a great sense of humor.

One-by-one, mourners spoke from their hearts, sharing their reflections. I was the last to speak. The short distance from my pew to the pulpit seemed like forever.

"A man that hath friends must show himself friendly: and there is a friend that sticketh closer than a brother," I reflected, citing Proverbs 18:24, as if I was back in "The Creek," sitting in Donald Keyser's religion class all over again.

"Galations 6:2 comes to mind, as well," I continued, looking towards the family, trying to comfort them while maintaining my composure.

"Bear ye one another's burdens, and so fulfil the law of Christ," I proclaimed, saying that "HE, as in Christ, wants us to love one another."

Carlton and I were not preachers by any means, but it was obvious that the spirituality in us was a common bond. These were the two scriptures that I felt most characterized my relationship with my beloved brother, classmate, friend, and teammate.

The charismatic, youthful looking Reverend Herbert C. Crump, Jr., from Carlton's adopted Rock Hill church, Freedom Temple Ministries, powerfully preached his eulogy, telling family and friends about *"A Job Well Done"* and the *"ABC's of a Successful Life."*

On January 17, 2009, while at the beautiful Pope Center, memories of Carlton were brought into focus. It had been nearly seven years since Carlton's death. "The number 7," "T" would probably have said, if he were here with us – "that's a good number: John Elway, Mickey Mantle and Kevin Johnson wore 7."

That day, while approaching the section reserved for former players and coaches to be recognized, I began to soak in how well the facility appeared to have been built, with its interior color scheme dominance of orange and black.

Simultaneously, I began to seek out people from my era, especially my teammates. Roddney McCants spotted and warmly greeted me. Afterwards, he introduced me to his wife; I introduced them to my cousin James, as well. It was always great to see Roddney, as we had a common denominator outside of basketball. My late Aunt Harriett Clark Marshall knew him and his parents because they attended the same Presbyterian Church down the street from her home on Seabrook Road in Fayetteville.

Upon further notice, I concluded that none of my NAIA National Runner-up teammates, managers, or coaches was there. I knew that "Coach" had a good excuse because he played a major role as caregiver for his wife, Barbara Roberts, who was suffering from Parkinson's disease.

"What would they say about this lovely facility?" I wondered, and began to one-by-one, reflect on what I knew of what they had become – all men now more than 50 years of age.

Roddney, cousin James, and I walked around the recently opened facility after we, with the exception of James, were part of the basketball alumni recognized at half-time at mid court of Pope's Gilbert Craig Gore Arena. We came upon the Campbell Hall of Fame Wall that is the centerpiece of the main entrance. "Some school officials were so excited back in 1977 that they talked of building "this" (referring to the new arena) then," I said, while studying the wall.

"Why isn't Sam up there?" I questioned, referring to the Hall of Fame Wall.

Having played with Laird and Whaley, I was pleased to see them displayed on the Wall before me.

"Oh, yeah!" Roddney acknowledged.

McCants never played with Sam Staggers but had seen him play during the evening counselors' games while attending Campbell's Summer Basketball School as a high school camper. I'm sure he learned more about Staggers from teammates after setting foot on campus as a freshman.

Campbell's planned entry into the NCAA in the 1977-1978 season might have been the impetus for the talk of a new arena as well.

"It might have been Wendell Carr or Fred McCall" retired Campbell Women's Basketball Coach Betty Jo Clary said, as we chatted in the corridor adjacent to Section 110.

This implied to me that both men – Carr, the former Campbell A.D. and Tennis Coach, and McCall, co-founder of Campbell's Summer Basketball School, along with Horace "Bones" McKinney, and former Men's Basketball Coach, were involved in planning the arena they would never live to see completed. McCall, with his warm hearty laugh, was also a long-time Campbell administrator and invented and patented the McCall Rebounder®, a practice tool for basketball.

"We've finally got the arena people talked about after returning from KCMO!" I thought, glancing at the sky, as I pulled out of the parking lot, and turned right onto Leslie Campbell Memorial Avenue, after the game. For years to come, many will continue to admire the large red brick physical testament to diligence, planning, and giving.

"Thirty-two years; 32 years since that special season of 1976-77 and our historic national championship run," I thought. "The number 32 – now that's a good number" I'm sure Carlton would have reminded me, if he wasn't in Heaven: "Earvin "Magic" Johnson, Sandy Koufax and Karl Malone."

Overhills

"To paraphrase John Milton, you don't know paradise until it's lost and now it seems that we've lost it twice…"

- Christopher "Kim" J. Elliman

On the snow-covered morning that Bird Song burned, people who were a part of the Overhills Estate and extended community, now spread nationwide, felt the sparks fading, as it reminded us of its famous past. Bird Song, the largest house on the compound, was built in 1962 by Avery Rockefeller to handle guests when Croatan, the main house, reached capacity.

Avery was the grandson of William Rockefeller and great nephew of John D. Rockefeller. This vacation home, located in the solitude of the North Carolina Sandhills, had 20 rooms; 14 were guestrooms, each one having its own private bathroom. Avery's great uncle, founder of Standard Oil Company, was once known as the "world's richest man," and left his mark on America with his systematic approach to philanthropy.

Local firefighters, led by Fort Bragg, would respond quickly, after getting the call 19 minutes past midnight, from its 911 Center on that chilly morning of February 4, 2009. They would work until midday among the snow-dusted longleaf pines, ensuring that a reoccurrence caused by possible smoldering flames would not flare up. The firefighters found the main section of the house destroyed, except for six chimneys, which they found still standing. These chimneys had hand-painted images of birds cemented to the mantle's bricks and these images were not damaged. According to Bryan Mims, a WRAL television reporter, "the tiles date back to the 18th century and the family painted images of trees and birds native to the Sandhills....thus inspiring the name Bird Song." Linda Carnes-McNaughton, a Fort Bragg history curator who had arrived at the scene, laid the ceramic pieces carefully on the cold moist ground. The tiles "are a testament for the Rockefellers' appreciation for the natural flora and fauna of this area," she stated.

Jeff D. Irwin, an anthropologist hired by Fort Bragg to document and chronicle the history of Overhills, somberly spoke to a reporter, saying that "it is a significant loss to their history (Rockefeller family) and the history of the property, and it is a significant loss for the Army, as well, because it will be a nice training asset for the Army." It seemed as if someone had died, comparable to the stunning loss of a human being - someone familiar.

Later that morning, Christopher "Kim" J. Elliman, grandson of Avery Rockefeller, great grandson of Percy Rockefeller (Yale University, Skull & Bones 1900), and son of Ann Rockefeller Elliman, would receive the news in New York via email.

The Fayetteville Observer (NC) quotes Mr. Elliman, a Yale University graduate, like many of his ancestors, and literature major, as saying:

"To paraphrase John Milton, you don't know paradise until it's lost and now it that we've lost it twice. First from selling and now from Bird Song burning down."

Bird Song, while tragically burned to the ground, still seemed to cling to its former stateliness. An aerial shot from a Raleigh television station's helicopter silently covered the ashes of the former 'sanctuary' – its expansive footprint, which enveloped an area of approximately 10,600 square feet and grounds where many "movers and shakers" once came to recreate, away from the harsh northern winters.

The difficult thing for me to accept is that the Overhills Estate "was", that it is no longer referred to in its present tense. The reality is that Fort Bragg did acquire it in 1997 and thus it is now referred to as the Northern Training Area (NTA IV), one of its largest training areas. Some, not having knowledge of the inner workings, would argue that the Rockefeller family did not have the full sense of the appreciation the community had for the Overhills Estate when they sold it to the U.S. military.

The community of Overhills, outside of the estate proper, remains today, outliving the latter's economic and social pulse, many years past its historical heydays of the 1920s and 1930s. Many of my ancestors, in particular, my maternal grandmother, provide an indirect connection for me to this former exclusive hunt club, farm, and estate. Years later, after the sale of the estate, Overhills' heart remains culturally fused to the heart of the community and it to the memory and its spirit.

Overhills, commonly referred to for much of the 20th century as the Rockefeller Estate, was always a curiosity to me. Secluded among its rural pines and wiregrass forest away from Highways 24/87, in the southwestern part of Harnett County's Johnsonville Township, it was a winter getaway for some of America's wealthiest families and their friends. Highways 24/87 was once the Old Western Plank Road that cut through the pine forests from Fayetteville to Bethania, a Moravian village on the outskirts of Salem (now a part of Winston-Salem).

Once a turpentine plantation in the 19th century, owned by a Scottish immigrant named Daniel McDiarmid, this 13,000-acre expanse was one of the many sources that helped North Carolina to become a leading exporter in the naval stores industry, which also included rosin, pitch and tar.

My maternal great-great-grandfather, Isaac Brinkley, was born circa 1820. His mother, my great-great-great-grandmother, is believed to have been named Nannie Brinkley and born in the 18th century. She was a slave mother on the plantation. My maternal great-grandmother, Harriet Brinkley Clark, was born a slave on the McDiarmid Plantation in 1849. She later would marry John A. Clark, a mullatto, who was six years her senior.

The plantation prospered until the death of Mr. McDairmid, but it was not without a price of damaging the spirit of many of my ancestors enslaved there. The fusion of cultures has not always been desirable and mutual. My maternal first cousin, Dr. Judith "Judy" Jackson, a retired educator and a Brinkley-Clark family historian, spent several years of her early childhood living in the Overhills community, outside of the Estate, with our grandparents. According to Judy, so painful was this period in its past that it was no secret "the Brinkleys hated the McDiarmids because of the mean treatment they had received from them. The old plantation house stood like a haunted reminder of slavery in the modern day North Carolina. This cruel home for the Brinkleys was situated off of the Old Plank Road…" Feelings had been brewing for a long time in my family. Arch McDiarmid, Daniel's ancestor, received a land grant from the King of England. That would have been in the 1700s. That's a lot of history!

"Why aren't we McDiarmids?" I had often wondered. According to family history, "their first master was a Brinkley family from the Wilmington area of North Carolina."

Although my grandfather Ike Clark was not a slave, so agonizing was this period in family history that once, while being asked about it by my cousin Judy, he bowed his head and said, "Let's not speak of this."

Photo: Dirt road leading to former Overhills Estate, Fort Bragg, NC

While growing up, I used to wonder how someone could amass such a fortune to have a southern playground – a compound so unlike anything in the immediate area – maybe, except Pinehurst. Donald Ross, a world - renowned golf course architect, himself a Scotsman, designed an eighteen-hole golf course, nine holes at a time and eight years apart. Most common people never even knew that such a signature landscape existed in those woods accessible from the main road, down a narrow dirt road. Yet, Overhills was not just a place where the rich and famous went to escape from their elite world by horseback riding, polo, rounds of golf, bird hunting, fox hunting, and socializing with others of similar social status. It was a community.

The Overhills Land Company was managed in a business-like manner. For the most part, it was self-sufficient. This sustainability was aided by farmers who grew fruits and vegetables and raised livestock, as well. The successful nursery where "Linden Oaks" were produced was a major revenue stream in the company's success.

IT'S THE RAILROAD, STUPID!

On a Saturday morning a little boy ran excitedly out the back door of his humble, one-story white-shingled home, bare feet and all, down the un-mortared cinderblock steps, past a washing machine, the type with the old wringer rollers, and into his back yard. It did not seem to matter to the little one about the sand kicked up loosely between his toes or the cool, crisp morning air punctuated with the fresh scent of pines. Neither did the faint steady picking sound of a red-cockaded woodpecker, excavating a cavity in a tree nestled in a lovely longleaf pine forest nearby, capture his attention. The only thing that mattered most, at that moment, was that another train was coming through.

This little boy mimicked the high-pitched sound of the moving train's whistle, emanating from the Atlantic Coast Line Railroad (ACLRR) tracks, as it cleared the rural village of Spout Springs in Johnsonville Township, just north of Overhills. He envisioned the train's conductor pulling the whistle chain. Accordingly, the little boy would respond, energetically yanking his imaginary chain with his left arm pumping and his fist clinched. The train was a couple of miles away, directly east through the pines, but the sounds were coming through in his ear, vividly, as if he were in that locomotive, pulling the real chain.

I am that little boy, fascinated by the sounds of the high-powered locomotive, with an insatiable curiosity of what cargo it would be carrying. Several decades earlier, the trains would have carried members, visitors, horses, and hounds to Overhills, upon its becoming a hunting club, and, eventually, a country resort. Then, it provided passenger service, as well.

In addition to transporting the members arriving at their "southern playground," these trains would often bring children of the family and guests. Some of these children would befriend the children of employees. Isaac Brinkley Clark and Clara Elizabeth Utley Clark both worked on the Estate, at some point, but did not live there.

Overhills and its previously named entities were founded by many men who had railroad interests. They had connections to the railroad industry, partly or indirectly. It might not have existed had it not been for the ACLRR spur connecting Fayetteville to Greensboro, North Carolina. This line, previously the Cape Fear and Yadkin Valley Railroad (CF&YV RR), served as transport for the many sportsmen via Greensboro. Before the hunting club days, the railroad was instrumental in transporting coal from Chatham County (near Greensboro) to Wilmington, North Carolina, on the Atlantic coast that would be used as fuel for Confederate blockade runner ships during the Civil War. Naval stores (turpentine, lumber, rosin, etc.) from the McDiarmid plantation were hauled down these tracks, too, a more feasible way to get exports to the sea compared to shipping down the Lower Little River and Cape Fear River. General John Gill, a Maryland capitalist and president of the CF&YV RR, became part owner of the "timbered property" in 1906, along with James T. Woodward, a New York banker, and other investors like William DuPont. The purchase marked the beginning of the Croatan Club of Manchester. Being the "boss'" of the railroad, it probably wasn't hard for General Gill to begin a railroad spur into the property in 1910. The dirt road leading southwest from the Overhills property to Pinehurst, as shown on earlier maps, indicates a relationship to the Tufts family, which established the world-renowned golfing resort in 1895. Leonard Tufts, a short-term co-owner of Overhills, employed Donald Ross at Pinehurst. Ross designed the first nine-hole course at Overhills in 1910. The additional nine-holes were completed by Ross in 1918.

Perhaps the most important relationship early on in the history of the property that had ultimate benefit to its long-term growth and prosperity was the one between Guilford County Sheriff James Francis Jordan and William Kent (Yale, Skull & Bones 1887). Jordan, of Greensboro, was a highly sought after expert hunting guide and sportsman, known for leading hunts in the Sandhills. Kent, a U.S. congressman, grew up in rural California and was a champion of conservative principles. He and his wife, Elizabeth Thacher Kent, were also associated with naturalist John Muir. They later donated the land that would become the redwood forest known as Muir Woods National Monument, north of San Francisco Bay. Kent married into a family of Yale graduates – father-in-law and Professor Thomas Anthony Thacher and brother-in-law Sherman Day Thacher (Yale, Skull & Bones 1835 and 1883, respectively).

The success of the 650-acre satellite operation of the Greensboro-based Lindley Nursery Company, located northeast of the former resort, is partly due to its close proximity to the railroad line. This favorable logistic provided an infrastructure to receive nursery stock and ship plants and shrubbery. The very popular Linden Oaks seedlings were produced there and shipped to Boston.

Photo: Nursery Road and Highway 24/87 (formerly the Plank Road), Fort Bragg, NC

Percy Rockefeller and fellow Bonesman W.A. Harriman purchased the Overhills Hunt Club in 1916. W.A. Harriman (Yale, Skull & Bones 1913) and his younger brother E.R. Harriman (Yale, Skull & Bones 1917) were heirs to their father E. H. Harriman's fortune. E.H. Harriman was a railroad baron and an executive with controlling interests in numerous major railroads like the Union Pacific Railroad, Central of Georgia, Illinois Central, Saint Joseph and Grand Island, and Southern Pacific; other holdings were the Pacific Mail Steamboat Company and Wells Fargo. The senior Harriman was a nature lover and was believed to have funded the largest and most famous nature expedition to Alaska in 1899, up to that time. This influence appears to have been a sustainable force on his siblings' appreciation of Overhills' rural environment. The Harriman brothers were members of the Overhills Shooting Syndicate, which terminated in 1932, and shareholders of the Overhills Land Company.

G.H. Walker, father-in-law of Prescott Bush (Yale, Skull & Bones 1917), was a member of the syndicate. Bush was the father of United States President George Herbert Walker Bush (Yale, Skull & Bones 1948) and grandfather of President George W. Bush (Yale, Skull & Bones 1968). Isabel Rockefeller, daughter of Percy and the former Isabel Stillman, was the bridesmaid in Prescott Bush and Dorothy Walker's wedding on August 6, 1921.

The railroads and people such as Percy Rockefeller and Avril Hammond, former governor of New York, affected my great uncle, Alfred Fuller, at an early age. Fuller, known for his wisdom and business prowess, lived to be 95 years old. Alfred was born in a log cabin in western Harnett County in 1895. He was six when he started school but was seven when he quit "to cut cardwood to pile up for the trains." His family allowed him to return to school the next year and he later graduated. During that era, completion of the seventh or eighth grade met the requirement for graduation. He married my dad's paternal aunt, Mary Gilchrist, and the two of them raised my father, Leonard Gilchrist, from an early age to adulthood because of his parents' untimely passing. Alfred Fuller's life would cross that of Percy Rockefeller in 1922, meeting in Harnett County, most likely on the estate, and traveling north. "I got in with the richest people in the United States," Uncle Alfred once told Darla Godwin, an area newspaper reporter, some sixty-eight years after his first meeting Percy

Rockefeller. Fuller, a World War I veteran, stated that he "took care of their (Rockefeller) horses, exercising them and grooming them." Knowing the Rockefellers allowed him to network and show his horse grooming and training skills to their wealthy friends.

In 1928, Uncle Alfred moved to Middlebrook, New York, and began employment with Avril Hammond, who was then governor of the state. He trained polo horses and worked under the tutelage of an English trainer. He described the Hammonds as railroad people, saying that "the trains would come right up to their door to get them. They were rich, rich." I believe that it was in the environment of some of the country's wealthiest families that Uncle Alfred developed his keen entrepreneurial sense, later becoming a large property owner, chicken and egg farmer, and landlord.

Then one day the trains went silent, fading down the tracks, forcing us to rely upon a memory of a bygone era. Years later, as an adult, the dots began to connect for me.

THE "UPSTARTS"

Granddaddy Ike, like many African Americans in his time, was a Lincoln Republican because President Abraham Lincoln freed the slaves and was from the Grand Ole Party. The story goes that he even voted for President Herbert Hoover, which he later regretted. In the Jim Crow era in which he lived most of his life, numerous blacks aligned politically with the more moderate and liberal northern republicans. This is unlike the political landscape of the post civil rights era to present day, especially in the American South. Granddaddy liked the "Rockefeller Republicans" and called the elite and their wealthy friends the "Upstarts." Granddaddy Ike, whose father was born free and whose paternal grandfather became a freedman over a score before "The War Between the States," was born in 1885, the year *The Rise of Silas Lapham* was published. William Dean Howells, once editor-in-chief of *Atlantic Monthly*, wrote this popular novel about three decades after the end of the Civil War. He was a close friend of Mark Twain, whose fictional novels also conveyed the realistic realm of American society. Like Twain, Howells was considered a literary American realist and portrayed the main character, Silas Lapham, as a successful American businessman who had arrived economically and was attempting to rise morally and socially.

Post-Civil-War American industrialists such as Rockefeller, Andrew Carnegie, and Jay Gould represented the nouveau riche, i.e., the rags to riches story. Researchers believe that *The Rise of Silas Lapham* satirized the demise of the old gentry elites in favor of the upstarts such as Rockefeller (John D.). Granddaddy Ike was a hard worker, whether at Fort Bragg or farming acres of tobacco, cotton, and other crops. Despite the huge contrast in their lives, he related to the work ethic of the upstarts.

On April 23, 1901, at 3:30 p.m. in the afternoon at St. Bartholomew's Church in Manhattan, New York, Percy Rockefeller and Isabel Stillman exchanged wedding vows. John W. Cross and Corliss E. Sullivan (both Yale, Skull & Bones 1900) would be among the six ushers to witness the occasion. These relationships would continue to grow beyond the Secret Society days in New Haven. These powerful men – Sullivan, a bank executive, and Cross, an architect, were also regular guests on winter visits to Overhills from the late 1920s to the early 1930s. Percy's remaining ushers, also members of Skull & Bones 1900, included James G. Greenway, Frank Dexter Cheney, and Frederick Baldwin Adams. It is not clear whether the remaining usher, William S. Coffin, was a member of the Secret Society.

It is now apparent that Overhills during the Percy Rockefeller decades was a magnet for Yale University alumni and his Bonesmen, especially members from year 1900 of Skull & Bones. Most men enjoyed use of the resort on their winter breaks. The surviving members established a trend of vacationing or "meeting" at Overhills during the late 1920s and early 1930s.

It is arguable that the members of the Overhills Land Company, their families, and the guests had an impact on the lives of the resident employees and extended community. During the height of the resort's era, it provided a suitable option compared to employment at Fort Bragg, the factories, timber, or agriculture.

After the Overhills Land Company era ended, the property became a Rockefeller family get-away and, eventually, a year-round home to Avery and Isabel Stillman Rockefeller. Its effect was less of an economic multiplier from that time forward. Obviously, the demand for workers to upkeep the estate was significantly less.

Overhills' presence did not transform the community from a sleepy rural village in the Upper Cape Fear River Valley of the Sandhills. The passage of time, North Carolina's rapid growth, and Base Realignment and Closing (BRAC) are the stimuli most responsible for the present economic growth cycle underway.

However, years later, when taken into perspective, the presence of Overhills left a positive impression on the greater community. In the area of race relations, as a community employer, Overhills became known as being fair and equitable – paying blacks and whites comparable wages for comparable work.

THE COMMON FOLKS

Willie "Henry" King, Ed McCarther, J.W. "Josh" Lofton, Walter Elliot… the number of laborers at Overhills goes on and on over the years. The previous names appear on the year-ending records for the Hunt Country and Kennel Department of the Overhills Hunt in 1927. The world might never know or care about these men (and women) but they were vital to the operations of the resort and estate. They were also my family's relatives and friends. Josh Lofton and Walter Elliot were well-known carpenters in the community. Josh Lofton also served as a long-term trustee at nearby Johnsonville A.M.E. Zion Church and was a seasoned leader when my father became Chairman of the Trustee Board in 1955. Their paths also crossed that of Percival Leonard Rosseau, as they built onto the garage at his Overhills' cottage studio. Rosseau, a native of Pointe Coupée Parish, Louisiana, was a world-famous artist, known for his Impressionist-influenced landscape painting style. Rosseau, in mid-life, moved to Paris in the mid-1890s to attend art school at Academie Julian. While at Julian, Rosseau, of French descent, gained notoriety as an artist who painted dogs.

When he returned to the United States nearly two decades later at the advent of World War I, he continued his passion for painting hunting dogs in the rural landscape, at Old Lyme, Connecticut. This is where his friendship with Percy Rockefeller began. This friendship would grow and Rockefeller eventually built Rosseau a studio and living quarters at the Overhills property, where he would have access to Rockefeller's dogs. It was at the studio that Rosseau painted *Two Setters in a Cooling Stream on the Grounds of Overhills, Fayetteville, North Carolina*, which sold for

$210,000 at Doyle New York's 9thAnnual Dogs in Art auction in 2007 – a new auction record.

The serenity of Overhills' piney woods moves me and I am not alone. The Spirit of ArgyllAmerica still runs through, around, and above it – expressing its resiliency, multi-culturalness and sustainable vision. We who have been informed can reminisce or faintly remember a culture and time many decades ago that fused several groups of people: young and old, rich and poor, black, white, and red, northerner and southerner, educated and uneducated, secret society or no society. Listen! Can't you hear the sound of the wiregrass being trampled on the ground by horses' hooves, setters crouching as they mark fowl, and hounds barking, chasing the foxes through the forest during the big hunt? Riders playing polo on the lawn; carpenters, cooks, horsemen, farmers, gardeners, and the like, busily working to keep the resort and hunt club in order. Imagine experiencing the pain of the Brinkleys and the benefits of the wealth of the McDiarmids up to the Civil War. Well! Perhaps the word "imagine" might be more realistic than "listen," especially considering that the resort is no more. No! Jokingly, we are not talking about the ghosts of Overhills. Yes! Seriously, we are talking about a spirit, the Spirit of ArgyllAmerica that made an imprint on a community, region, and state.

THE VISION

James Stillman Rockefeller, the former President and Chairman of CitiBank, lived to be 102 years old. Mr. Rockefeller was the grandson of William Rockefeller. A U.S. Olympic medal winner (Paris 1924) and captain of his Yale University rowing team, James loved Overhills and Long Valley Farm, with its bald cypress-gum swamp, as did others in his family. This Phi Beta Kappa graduate and World War II veteran spent many of the formative years of his youth horseback riding, swimming, and enjoying the recreational bounty that these two properties had to offer.

James' love for nature arguably led the New York City-born banker to bequeath the historic Long Valley Farm, all 1,420 acres, to the North Carolina Conservancy in 2004, upon his death. The Conservancy has since prepared the farm, which includes a 100-acre lake, and transferred it to the North Carolina State Parks system in 2010. It is now a part of

Carver's Creek State Park, located in northern Cumberland County, near Spring Lake. Carver's Creek will focus on the protection of the longleaf pine ecosystem.

Because of James Stillman Rockefeller's selfless vision, others will now be able to share in the beauty and tranquility of what once fascinated him as be progressed through the cycles of life on frequent visits to Long Valley Farm.

7

The Sandhills
The Tufts and the Boyds

"Maybe at some future time the pine tree will be given its rightful credit for the part it played in the lives of our forefathers."

- Malcolm Fowler, *They Passed This Way*

As I drove south from the once thriving rural town of Cameron, down U.S. Highway 1 in Moore County, North Carolina, I listened to songs from *The Air I Breathe*, the smooth, sweet and soulful contemporary gospel jazz CD of Atlanta's Antonio Allen. The nationally recognized composer and musician has become known for his ability as a soprano-saxophonist and for his praise and worship songs. I became focused on one particular song of many special ones. The multi-talented Allen, known for his "breathless" holding of a note for what seems eternity, played the moving instrumental rendition of the original Michael W. White song (written by Marie Barnett), "Breathe."

As I turned right on Midland Road towards Pinehurst, I replayed the song in my car's CD player, immersed in the melodic sounds coming from its speakers while soaking up a fresh new October morning. I continued meditating about what the song meant to me personally, and that, ironically, it was unrefined opportunity and God's air, the air that breezed through the longleaf pines of the Sandhills, that led many wealthy people to the area around the turn of the 20th century – people like James Walker Tufts and James Yeomans Boyd.

It had been several decades since my last visit to the Pinehurst area. The splendor of the beautifully landscaped median, well-kept yards, plush Bermuda green fairways, and Donald Ross designed golf courses which lined the thoroughfare reminded me of just how special this place is. Knowing the lyrics, I continued to hum the song, as a gentle, sweet spirit allowed them to minister to me.

> *"This is the air I breathe*
> *This is the air I breathe*
> *Your holy presence living in me…"*

People used to describe the Sandhills of North Carolina as the "sand barrens." In geological terms, the Sandhills, an area 1,500 square miles, is a transitional point between the state's Coastal Plain and Piedmont Plateau areas. It is the result of the merger of tides and wind on an ancient ocean shoreline, running through the area. Before the development of the naval stores industry, the Sandhills was home to an abundant virgin forest. The sand barrens was an area depleted of the longleaf pines from within this vast dense forest when James Walker Tufts stepped off the train on the Raleigh and Augusta Rail Line in the peaceful little Moore County village he would name Pinehurst in 1895. He was one of the many well-to-do outsiders "who came by train and chose to remain."

Tufts, a soda fountain magnate from Massachusetts, intended to leverage the mild, healthy climate by building a resort. The naval stores industry helped North Carolina to prosper in the 19th century. Yet, it became apparent that industry leaders did not have a comprehensive plan regarding the sustainability of the longleaf pine. This lack of foresight left the area cleared of thousands of acres of trees, thus commonly referred to as the "pine barrens." Tufts purchased 6,000 acres for $1 dollar per acre. He hired Frederick Law Olmsted, by then world-renowned for his landscape architectural design of New York City's Central Park and Asheville, North Carolina's Biltmore House. Olmsted designed Pinehurst to resemble a New England village.

Tufts had the vision. Originally, Pinehurst was to be a resort where Northern working men and women could recuperate from diseases such as tuberculosis (TB) in a less harsh and healthier environment. Tufts began to market the resort to Boston physicians. The American Clinical and Climatological Association or the "Climatological" was birthed in 1884 and influenced societies worldwide with its climato-therapeutic ideas. In the early days of the Climatological, doctors and scientists focused on tuberculosis, believing that it could best be treated by living in an appropriate climate – much like the Sandhills.

Ironically, Tufts' business plan did not work as envisioned, as the resort did not attract working people. Additionally, many were uncomfortable with the thought of being around TB patients as the public's awareness of the often-fatal disease grew. However, its lack of initial success as a wellness resort proved to be a benefit, as it soon transformed into a major golfing haven.

My paternal great uncle, James Herbert Frye, lived to be 100 years old and was two when Mr. Tufts hired Ross, the Scotsman, to design several golf courses, including Pinehurst No.2, in 1900. Frye worked for Pinehurst, Inc. for 40 years. During his employment at Pinehurst, renowned golfers such as Byron Nelson, Sam Snead, and Ben Hogan would win here. Arnold Palmer would also frequent the links as a college student and golfer at Wake Forest, located near Raleigh, at that time. Babe Didrikson Zaharias would hit the links here, winning the 1947 Women's North and South Amateur and continue to break gender barriers, along with her friend Peggy Kirk Bell.

I remember my uncle as a slim man with good posture, distinguished by his wire-rim glasses, good looks, and contagious smile. I can still hear him in my childhood memory, however faintly, sharing a hearty cackling laugh with my father, his sister's child.

Known to his nieces and nephews as "Uncle Herbert," he was a pillar in his community. He and his wife Bessie lived in unincorporated Jackson Hamlet, wedged between Aberdeen and Pinehurst, from 1921 until their deaths. My cousin Carol Henry, my uncle and aunt's granddaughter, has accepted the role as a respected community leader and shepherds Jackson Hamlet Community Action, having assumed the reins from Oneal Russ.

Uncle Herbert was not the only pillar in the surrounding community. Many families helped to establish Jackson Hamlet. Thanks to C.E. Pleasants and his wife Bette, the predominately black community was created when, in 1908, the Pleasants deeded land to James Jackson, a self-employed toolmaker, Saint Paul Missionary Baptist Church, and its trustees. People like the Gaines family, the Cottons, and the McRaes, to name a few, were considered pioneers in this minority community.

During the 20th century, African-Americans migrated from all over the lower Piedmont region and southeastern North Carolina to work what were considered "good jobs" at Pinehurst. As the resort grew into a global golfing destination, it provided employment for maids, groundsmen, caddies, cooks, and other laborers. Ida Mae Murchison, a resident of Jackson Hamlet, was very active in her community and one of the longest serving workers ever at the resort.

Both Jackson Hamlet's Cabin in the Pines and the more upscale Ambassador Club were magnets for many leading entertainers during World War II, drawing crowds from all over the Sandhills to see the likes of Sam Cooke, James Brown, Louis Jordan, Cab Calloway, etc.

Uncle Herbert worked in the dairy, well known nationally and internationally for its Ayrshire cattle, and in the garage during his career that would span four decades. Despite Pinehurst's success, these laborers were resilient and faced an ambiguous working and social environment, embraced as laborers but not allowed equal access to its facilities. Jackson Hamlet, a predominately-black community located between Aberdeen and Pinehurst, was the community of choice for many of the resort workers. Midway and Taylortown, which was eventually incorporated, were adjacent communities, among others, where laborers lived.

Coincidentally, the sustainability of Pinehurst, once referred to by some as Pinalla or Tuftstown, may have started when James Walker Tufts hired Olmsted's Boston land design firm. Gwilym S. Brown, a *Sports Illustrated* writer, in Pinehurst two weeks before the start of the National Amateur Golf Championship in 1962, wrote about Pinehurst in *SI's* September 10 edition. He described the resort's origins as miraculous, with Tufts buying several thousand acres of "desert." Brown said that Tufts

"called his little village Pinehurst because a hurst is a mound or piece of rising ground, usually a sandy one. Early visitors scanned the arid waste around them and announced that

they could understand the hurst part of the name very well but for the life of them could not see how pines could be connected with the place." (Brown, Gwilym S. The Southern Resort of a Proper Bostonian. Sports Illustrated. September 10, 1962.)

Tufts, an astute businessman, listened to his customers. Olmsted's designs ordered 200,000 trees and shrubs, fifty thousand of them from overseas. They included longleaf pine, dogwood, holly, and magnolias, laid out in concentric circles, as the streets extended outward from the New England-like village greens.

Leonard Tufts, son of James Walker Tufts, although quite busy growing a golf resort, which included a state of the art dairy, had a sustainable interest in the trees, especially the longleaf pine. This was quite evident by the detail that Warren H. Manning, president of Warren H. Manning, Offices, Inc., used to communicate his observations of the longleaf pine in a typed letter to Mr. Tufts, dated February 3, 1923.

Pinehurst's beauty is the result of the vision of both Olmsted and Manning, giants in landscape architecture. Olmsted started the vision and Manning implemented it. Manning was the single landscape architect for the Tufts family for 46 years.

"This letter is a memorandum concerning the observations on Long Leaf Pine that we made together. I am enclosing an extra copy so that you can make corrections and return it to me if you will.

The Long Leaf Pines that were seedlings in 1907 and dug with a spade to retain a deep ball and usually a tuft of wire grass, were planted in the Village Green in 1907, that is, fifteen years ago. Some of the trees have failed but the tuft of wire grass persists where they were planted to such an extent that a nearly accurate account of the number of first trees could be made. These trees now vary in height, from about two feet to about thirty-five feet in height, some having a diameter of 10 inches. One tree that was 2½ inches in diameter, that was blown over, was found to be

18 ft. in height to the tip of the leaves.

...It thus appears that transplanted trees grow much more rapidly than trees left in place, and that trees that are one foot high in the wild average about seven to eight years of age, the first three years being very slow. Usually after the 7th or 8th years they begin to grow rapidly. It is also obvious from the above notes that some trees will live many years without making much of any growth."

Yours very truly,

Warren H. Manning Offices, Inc.

By President

(Tufts Archives)

It was Richard Tufts, grandson of the founder of Pinehurst, who cemented its legacy and became a leader of the American golf movement in the 20th century. Known as "Mr. Golf" and "The Man Who Was Pinehurst," Richard and family shareholders sold Pinehurst's many assets to Diamondhead Corporation in 1970 for $9.2 million. Many historians say that, in retrospect, this represented a marked change in Pinehurst's character.

WHERE DID MY LONGLEAF PINE GO?

Located in Southern Pines, North Carolina, the historic and picturesque James Boyd house, its central structure a two-story red-brick colonial with a gabled roof and double chimney, sat prominently in the distance, adjacent the gardens. As Kim Hyre, a Weymouth Woods park ranger, and I turned to enter the 900-acre nature preserve, I reflected on this being the site where the younger Boyd, James' grandson, wrote *Drums* with the help of his wife Katherine. Many literary experts consider it the best Revolutionary War novel ever. One would surmise that he gained inspiration from this natural setting, as he refers to the pine tree and turpentine, a by-product of the plentiful longleaf pine, within the book's first two paragraphs.

> *"A FIRE BLAZED in the deep, clay-plastered fireplace; logs of North Carolina pine dripped turpentine in the wave of flame and sent up scrolls of clotted smoke to join the night. His short coat and his kilt were brown, his square beard was brown,... Outside, the rustle of the pines crept by in long, low waves which came from the Atlantic to the eastward and crossed the forests of the Province on tossing tops to die away against the mountains in the west."*

Photo: James Boyd House and Gardens at Weymouth Center, NC

With the skill of someone who knew the woods as well as the lines in the palms of her hands, Kim, a native of Huntington, West Virginia, drove through the area on this cold, overcast January afternoon, in the department's white pickup truck, headed towards the "elder in the forest."

Privileged was I to be a passenger, gazing curiously out my window, as we gently rode over the ridges, the ruts, the clumps of brown dry leaves, and the sandy and sometimes muddy soil. Unexpectedly, we paused to see the second largest longleaf pine tree in North Carolina. This tree, believed to be born in 1550, is stunningly beautiful, and its size easily dwarfed all the trees around it.

"It's so wide, you and I together, could not wrap our arms around it," said Kim.

We continued on, stopping in an opening.

"Look to your right. That stand of trees over there with the crowns is some of the most mature in the forest," she informed me.

I could sense that what I was witnessing was one of the marquis moments of a lifetime. Never before had I recalled seeing longleaf pines that looked like that, flat tops thickening out – its trunk, thick and tall. Finally, we arrived at our destination.

While continuing to ride through the forest I could not help but notice the black soot on the pine bark of the trees, apparently the results of a controlled burn. Dormant wiregrass lay sleeping all around them.

As Kim brought the truck to a stop, she turned slightly to me and said suddenly, "We often think of fire as the enemy of the forest but it is not."

Kim's wise and beloved friend Charlotte Orr Gantz, author and centenarian, both asks and answers the following question in her book, *Discovering the Forest:*

> "Why should there be such burning? The fact is that the longleafs and the hardwoods are a never-ending battle. If the oaks and other hardwoods were to win, the pines would disappear and with them would go many of the plants and animals that have grown up in this particular forest and that would die without it. So more is at stake than just the life of the longleafs. Gone would be the rare red-cockaded woodpecker, the fox squirrel, the Pine Barrens tree frog, as well as wiregrass, picture plants, orchids, arbutus and great numbers of other wildflowers."

As we stepped out of the vehicle and into the wide dirt path, Kim observed that the forest seemed unusually quiet. We both nodded in agreement that the animals must know that a major snowstorm was coming, predicted to arrive in a few hours. With my sense of direction having caught up with me, I suddenly realized that we were underneath the stand of trees seen from afar, only minutes before. With confidence, Kim pointed me in the direction of what I had traveled from my home in Georgia to see.

"This tree is 462 years old," Kim stated, and began to tell me how this fact was determined. "The oldest longleaf pine tree, on record, in the United States!" Kim proudly exclaimed.

"It's not as beautiful as the large tree that we passed on the way," I said, moving closer to the tree, which appeared to be leaning slightly and charred around half of its base.

Kim nodded a little, as if in agreement. Nevertheless, I was awed to be in its presence. A few feet away, we spotted a longleaf pine seedling, which had no trunk yet, its green, long pine needles spiraling over like an umbrella of "heavy green grass." This formed a startling visual contrast. Evidence of the environmentally protected and clannish red-cockaded woodpecker was nearby as Kim directed my attention to two pine trees that had round holes bored into them, at about the middle of the tree.

While standing in front of the very old longleaf pine, my thoughts turned to how lucky it was to have survived. I was amazed at the abundance of dormant plant life found on its small sandy hills. Here I was, almost daunted to be among these longleaf pines, which were rooted in the sandy soil covered by wiregrass and turkey and blackjack oaks.

I closed my eyes and imagined what it had experienced over time.

It would have been 1548 when a pinus palustris, Latin for longleaf pine, germinated in the wiregrass of a tall, thick virgin forest in the Sandhills of North Carolina. Twenty-two years earlier, Spanish explorer and slave trader Lucan Vasquez de Aylion would have attempted to settle – unsuccessfully - the lower Cape Fear, its river once referred to by the Native American Indians as the "Sapona." Four years before the seedling would take deep root, Hernando De Soto would have led an expedition, looking for gold to the west, in the North Carolina mountains. He would not have seen the enterprising value in what the British would later see – the trees. There, De Soto would have encountered the Cherokee. The seedling would have become a sapling, and, ultimately, a tree. From De Soto to today, what must it have known, what stories it could tell.

Photo: Oldest longleaf pine, on record, in U.S. at Weymouth Woods Preserve, NC

I wondered, silently, "Why did this tree survive, and live to have the distinction of being the oldest longleaf pine in a state with millions of trees from Murphy to Kitty Hawk, from Mount Airy to Kings Mountain, and in a greater longleaf region that stretches from southwest Virginia to east Texas and south to Florida?" Appreciatively, I glanced over to where Kim was standing, full of the wealth of knowledge that I had soaked up.

Could this tree have seen William Bartram? Bartram, an American-born 18th century explorer and naturalist, still incites the curiosity of others many years after emotionally documenting his observations in what is known as *Bartram's Travels*. Bartram journeyed through seven southern states, including the Sandhills and Coastal Plain of Eastern North Carolina, during the mid 1770s. "What Bartram saw" is the statement the author, Lawrence S. Earley, makes in his book *Looking for Longleaf,* as he describes, in full detail, the sights, the sounds, and the feel of interacting with a great virgin longleaf pine forest. A young and vibrant Bartram described hearing the sounds emanating from the treetops as "the solemn symphony of the steady Western breezes, playing incessantly, rising and falling through the thick and wavy foliage."

This longleaf pine was almost 200 years old when the Thistle, the most notable immigrant ship to bring Highlanders from Argyllshire, Scotland, to the shores of Eastern North Carolina, landed in Wilmington in 1739. It, no doubt, witnessed their migration as they settled further inland, making the Sandhills their home. So impressed were the Scottish Highlanders of what they "kenned" or gained knowledge of in their adopted land, reference to the longleaf pine would soon enter the lyrics of a famous Gaelic lullaby, Dèan calablan sámhach (Go to sleep peacefully).

"…Gur h-ann an America tha sinn an-dràst'
An iomall na coille nach teirig gu bràth…".

"…We are now in America
At the edge of the never-ending forest…"

This tree knows how fortunate it was to have survived, as many trees nearby became the lumber for homes or businesses. Its neighbor, the Malcolm Blue Farm, now serving as the western boundary to Fort Bragg, is south of Weymouth Woods, down Bethesda Road, in Aberdeen. Malcolm, a descendant of Scottish immigrants, was a very large landowner who became wealthy in the naval stores industry, particularly turpentine and rosin. As was often the case during that era among prosperous white Southerners, he owned seven slaves. Malcolm attended Bethesda Presbyterian Church, which conducted services in both Gaelic and English and had a slave gallery prior to the Emancipation Proclamation. Midway is a predominately black community ceded from the Malcolm Blue Estate. It intrigues me still that many of my 18th and 19th century ancestors in North Carolina's Argyll Colony, who originally spoke the African Bantu language, may have spoken Gaelic as well as anyone before transitioning solely to English.

During the 19th and 20th centuries, with the advent of the plank road cutting through the region and increased national and international demand for naval stores, thousands of acres of pine forests were devastated.

Many of my maternal ancestors in the Sandhills region worked on tree or turpentine plantations like the McDairmid's as boxers, lumbers, and sawyers before the Civil War. While enslaved, they helped the Tar Heel State earn its infamous nickname. After the War between the States, when the white tree farmers could no longer take advantage of forced labor, many blacks continued the same occupation but under much different circumstances. Meanwhile, the sandy ridges became more barren of pines, and many of the trees that remained were not healthy ones, often because of less than desirable turpentine boxing cuts.

Miraculously, the tree deep in the Moore County forest, now about 350 years old, was spared from being the next resource. Then James Yeomans Boyd, a Pennsylvania coal merchant, capitalist, and State Railroad Commissioner, and his wife, Eleanor Gilmore Herr Boyd, came to Moore County because of their appreciation for the woods and the opportunity to buy cheap land. They bought the tract of land that included a pine forest where this tree was firmly rooted. If this tree could talk, it would tell them the history of the devastation of the region all around them. This tree would tell them about "death by a thousand cuts," which describes the long destruction of North America's greatest conifer forest, over many decades. More specifically, if this tree could talk, it would thank not just Mr. James Y. Boyd but his daughter, Mrs. Helen Boyd Dull. Thomas P. Ivy, author of *The Long Leaf Pine,* wrote that it was Mrs. Dull who tugged at her father's heart to buy the land where this elder among trees now sits:

> "...By chance, in 1904, Mrs. Dull, with her father, the late Mr. James Boyd, of Harrisburg, Pa., came to visit Southern Pines. In driving through the pine forest on Weymouth Heights they came upon trees by the roadside that were boxed for turpentine. Mrs. Dull was so grieved at this seeming desecration that she urged her father to buy the land and stop the mutilation of the trees. He acted that same day, and to that tract other tracts were added from time to time until the present Weymouth Estate of 1500 acres was acquired, all of which comes within the original Shaw entries."

More than 365 years after the birth of this magnificent tree, then standing 110 feet high with a diameter of 2' 4", considered the oldest long leaf pine in the state of North Carolina, Mr. Ivy shared his thoughts with a group of men and women in Southern Pines about the same tree. He meticulously describes the tree's evolution, in first person, as if a camera's video footage had patiently compressed it:

> *"When I first flew out from my mother cone I alighted on a thick cover of needles. There I lay apparently lifeless for nearly a year, until in late winter a large buck, who was feeding around under my ancestors, stepped upon me by chance and pressed me down against the bosom of the earth. With the coming of spring I began to feel the sensation of life. There was a swelling of the embryo into a force that sent it through the seed-leaves and behold, I was born. In those days, there was no prohibition and my first desire was for drink. So I dispatched my small rootlets out in every direction for mineral and drove my taproot downward for drink. All my baby days and childhood were thus occupied, all my activities being underground rather than above. But at the end of four years I changed my program, seeking with light and heat to carry myself upward on the foundations already laid…Three times during this period I almost despaired of my life. One year was so dry I nearly died from thirst and twice forest fires raged that charred my lower body unmercifully. All this you could read in the smaller ring of annual growth for those years from a cross section of my body…"*

Such empathy this tree must have felt for other pines not so fortunate. During the 1920s, the Floridian poet Anne McQueen, in her poem "The Cry Of The Pines" expressed in stanzas selected below the plight of the endangered longleaf pines, in an almost animated way, with great feeling, as they sorrowfully communicate with each other.

Listen! The great trees call to each other:
"Is it come your time to die, my brother?"
And through the forests, wailing and moaning,
The hearts of the pines, in their branches groaning:
"We die, we die!"

All through the land are the forests dying.
One piece of silver a tree-life buying;
Listen! The great trees moan to reach other:
"The ax has scarred us too, my brother"-
"We die, we die!"

In 1957, some four hundred and nine years later, the North Carolina General Assembly passed S.B. 305, a poem or song referred to as "A Toast" to North Carolina and written in 1904 by Leonora Martin and Mary Burke Kerr. The state song, approved in 1927, includes the same lyrics and is titled "The Old North State."

"Here's to the land of the Longleaf pine,
The summer land where the sun doth shine
Where the weak grow strong and the strong grow great,
Here's to "Down Home, "the Old North State!

Here's to the land of the cotton bloom white,
Where the scuppernong perfumes the breeze at night,
Where the white southern moss and Jessamine mate,
'Neath the murmuring pines of the Old North State!"

Many people give toasts in celebration of events such as achieve-ments, anniversaries, birthdays, engagements, good health, friendship, and their reasons continue. You name it and there has probably been a toast in honor of it. But… a toast to what would later become law as the state tree by way of the North Carolina State Legislature passing H.B. 10 Chapter

151

Ernest R. Gilchrist

41 in 1963?

In North Carolina's State Toast, the words longleaf pine or pines are mentioned in the first verse of the first stanza and the last verse of the second stanza. A romantic, almost symbiotic relationship evolved over the centuries in how people felt about the longleaf pine. This relationship is expressed in almost human qualities.

Because of the commercialization of the longleaf pine and its by-products, which once launched an exports-leading naval stores industry, the term "pine barrens" became a household expression. By the beginning of the 20th century, when Martin and Kerr penned the lyrics, this love affair was in full bloom. The longleaf pine, once considered a sustainer of life, touched so many lives, becoming the lifeline of the 19th century economy. Ivy, also a forest engineer, expressed society's relationship with the longleaf pine in this manner:

> *"But as individual human beings we are indebted to long leaf pine for the comfort and shelter it has extended to two-thirds of the nation. Long leaf pine is a paying guest in every house east of the Rocky Mountains. It is to be found in the desk of every school house. Non-sectarian, it speaks from every pulpit and kneels around every altar. It is the main supporting timber of every mill and factory in New England. Not a train east of the Rocky Mountains could move if long leaf pine forbade, and not a steamer could sail from an Atlantic or Gulf port. Long leaf pine created the wealth and built the cities of Norfolk, of Wilmington, of Charleston, of Jacksonville, of Mobile, of New Orleans and Galveston. To these cities and states and citizens everywhere in the Union long leaf pine appeals to be permitted to live and continue to give wealth, happiness and prosperity to its millions of beneficiaries."*

"Maybe at some future time the pine tree will be given its rightful credit for the part it played in the lives of our forefathers," North Carolina author Malcolm Fowler expressed, several years prior to "The Toast" being formally recognized.

In Fowler's era, his use of the words "our forefathers" perhaps was not truly inclusive. It is a question for history as to the spirit of how Fowler might have intended it. More importantly and indisputably is the fact that "our forefathers," across races, cultures, and ethnicities helped to make the state known as the Tar Heel State.

I imagined seeing my ancestors, as Olmsted may have seen them, the Pinehurst resort laborers, the Tufts and the Boyds, McQueen, Martin, Kerr, Earley, Gantz, and those who remain nameless. All of that! Still a little intimidated, I gazed upwards again, snapping pictures of this great tree, and for a moment, I felt connected. I felt the Spirit of ArgyllAmerica, that is, man's connection to God and nature in one. I imagined hearing the rustle of the pines, the moans and murmurs of the trees and the treetops, and Bartram's symphony, telling me in praise:

> *"How great is our God*
> *Sing with me*
> *How great is our God,*
> *And all will see*
> *How great*
> *How great,*
> *How great is our God"*
> *(Chris Tomlin).*

8

C-5A On A Sunny, Sunny Day

"... I'm a big bird in the sky all will jump and some will die, off to battle we will go to live or die, hell I don't know..."

- Excerpt from Hail O' Infantry

It seems ironic, in retrospect, that the United States military should choose an area of the country heavily inhabited by the ancestors of the Highland Scots to establish Fort Bragg in 1919. Historically, going back to Scotland, the Highlanders had a militaristic culture. Although often characterized as a very sensitive people, both men and women were used to wearing arms and stayed prepared for mass battle or dueling.

My African ancestors, the Bantu speaking Bube of Equatorial Guinea's Bioko Island and the Tikar people of Cameroon, were also strong fighters, with the former defending their isolated extinct volcanic island, located in the Gulf of Guinea, for centuries against European slave traders.

"C-5A on a sunny, sunny day! C-5A on a sunny, sunny day!" I would gleefully exclaim, repeatedly, when I saw one of those mammoth mechanical birds.

As a child growing up in western Harnett County, I always got so excited when the huge aircraft flew over my family home that I created my very own greeting for it. I was 12 or 13 years old when the Lockheed C-5A Galaxy, a large high-wing cargo aircraft, started to fly out of neighboring Pope Air Field. Its hard-surface runway was extended to 7,500 feet in 1970 for C-5A aircraft. The sheer magnificence of the C-5A both fascinated and awed me on those beautiful sunny Carolina blue afternoons. The C-5A's boldness, as it pierced the skies, made me feel proud to be an American, even as a young teenager.

The windowpanes of our small frame house shook with each round fired by the powerful guns. "Dud-dud-dud-dud, dud-dud-dud-dud!" I would hear and feel, repeatedly. In the background, I could hear the steady staccato of high-powered weapons being fired by solders on the artillery range, about 20 to 25 miles southwest, deep into the Sandhills, through the pines. I have fond childhood memories of placing my ear to the ground to hear the reverberation echoing from the distance.

"Iron Mike," the airborne trooper, now stands "watching, waiting and alert" near Randolph and Armistead Streets. I remember, arguably, when Fort Bragg's most prominent symbol, the 15-foot statue, was at Knox and Bragg Boulevard. Personally, I preferred the original location because it was much more accessible in the post 9/11 era. Today, non-military people, like me, do not often get a chance to see "Iron Mike" unless they are civil service employees, contractors, or vendors. The statue was named after Major General "Iron Mike" Healey, one of the early officers of the Special Forces Groups.

Perhaps what binds the military, its culture, and the region's culture can be found in the meter and rhyme of the cadence. The discipline, the unity of the brotherhood, the singularity of purpose, the camaraderie, all locked in step.

"One, Two, Three, Your Left, Hoo ah! One, Two, Three, Four" the Army Airborne Rangers repeat as they run, seeking a flawless rhythm.

A casual observer cannot get caught up in the visual imagery of these well conditioned soldiers, moving in step like a collective human locomotive, for the power lies in their words.

"Up in the morning, outta the rack
Greeted at dawn with an early attack
First Sergeant rushes me off to chow
But I don't need it anyhow
Hail O' Hail O' Infantry

Ernest R. Gilchrist

Queen of battle follow me
An airborne ranger's life for me
O' nothing in this world is free..."

The key underlying theme is that for a soldier there are many uncertainties. Life or death is not promised, but they must all be prepared for battle – to fight for freedom, which has a cost. This resiliency, steeped through tradition through the centuries, is what connects the armed forces and promotes multiculturalism. Why? No matter where you come from or your socioeconomic background, color, or ethnicity, in today's military, you are all the same as a soldier.

It's not "Iron Mike," the Special Forces and the Green Berets, the number of generals assigned to the post, the mammoth airplanes of my childhood flying over eastern North Carolina skies, or the Army's powerful guns that define the military's role in ArgyllAmerica. I contend that it is the pursuit of racial harmony that tends to exist in regions of the United States where the armed forces are an important part of the community's fabric. Fort Bragg, one of the largest military installations in the country, is not alone in the value system embraced by most of the men and women who serve there. However, its cultural impact on the region helps to more positively reinforce the overall desire for a more harmonious multicultural environment and resilient work ethic.

Based on the fascinating research of Charles C. Moskos and John S. Butler, the nation's leading sociologists on race relations in the military, blacks or Afro-American soldiers had been more prone than whites to have experienced racism in the armed forces structure. Moskos and Butler stressed that the term African-American "seems to emphasize more the uniquely American aspects of the black experience, an experience that has been a defining quality of America's core culture that Africa has never been." Nevertheless, blacks expressed that the military life, comparatively speaking, was more favorable than life as a civilian.

Moskos and Butler present many takeaways or lessons for all Americans. Their findings suggest that the "... Army's multicultural uniculture--and the fact that this uniculture is Afro-Anglo--has been an unquantifiable contributor to its success in race relations. American society sorely needs some similar amalgamation of the two dominant cultures."

These 12 lessons, first developed by Army social scientists, are extremely frank and revealing. I will not repeat the entire dozen here, but it is interesting to note that the first lesson shares that "Blacks and Whites Will Not View Opportunity and Race Relations the Same Way." Despite the Army's being credited by many as "the most successfully racially integrated institution in American society, blacks and whites still have disparate views of equal opportunity."

Moskis and Butler seemed to have uncovered in their findings the answer to the Army's resilient work ethic by sharing that the "Army experience emphasizes the correlation between reward and effort (as opposed to reward and race)." Like what gives much credence to their reporting, the two sociologists often compare opinions, not only those of black and white soldiers but those of black and white civilians.

Give'em Hell, Harry! was the name of a one-man stage play, starring James Whitmore and focusing on the presidency of Harry S. Truman, that Brian McNeill and I had the pleasure to see at Ford's Theatre in 1974. We were there for Close Up, a highly recognized educational program where high school students from all over the nation participate in a "close up" experience with democracy in action in Washington, D.C.

Known as a plain speaking Midwesterner in real life, Truman, when responding to a vocal supporter at an Illinois campaign stop, once said, "I don't give them hell, I just tell the truth about them and they think it's Hell."

President Truman's courage and his unwavering boldness significantly influenced civil rights in our nation. Many of his decisions broke the walls of segregation in the military, Fort Bragg notwithstanding.

Yes, 1948 was a critical year among years that helped to move the United States forward. It was a year after Jackie Robinson broke the color line in major league baseball and became a Brooklyn Dodger. The Harlem Globetrotters, an all black basketball team known throughout as entertainers, defeated all white George Mikan and the Minneapolis Lakers in a serious battle that had more societal implications than anything else. Supreme Court decisions such as *Sipuel v. Board of Regents of Oklahoma University* and *Shelly v. Kraemer* helped to remove barriers which denied or restricted people regarding housing on grounds of race. It was also the year that Truman presented his civil rights message to the U.S. Congress.

From the Lincoln Memorial, less than eight months before, he became the first American President to address the National Association for the Advancement of Colored People (NAACP).

A. Philip Randolph was among many strong black civil rights leaders who had Truman's ear. Randolph started out offering counsel to President Franklin D. Roosevelt to end discrimination and segregation in the Armed Forces. Randolph, having his hands on the pulse of the black community, had informed both presidents on numerous occasions of the intention of African American youth to resist the draft law.

These occurrences, in addition to unfortunate racially motivated incidences across the nation involving military personnel or veterans, led Truman to sign two Executive Orders in 1948. Executive Order 9980 prohibited discrimination in the federal government and required merit-based employment only.

Executive Order 9981 established that "there shall be equality of treatment and opportunity for all persons in the armed services without regard to race, color, religion, or national origin."

These significant events indicated to Randolph that the much talked about "March on Washington" that he had threatened for much of a decade was no longer necessary, as the country's leadership was sincere.

The future of ArgyllAmerica, the place, which is the greater Fayetteville-Fort Bragg, North Carolina region, may be on the cusp of a major sea change, one unseen perhaps since the impact that World War II had on the military, commercial, and cultural hub of the Sandhills.

Timothy "Brian" McNeill, current Chairman of the Harnett County Board of Commissioners as well as Chairman of the Base Realignment and Closing (BRAC) Regional Task Force (RTF), was a child-hood friend and schoolmate at Olivia, North Carolina's Benhaven School. "Brian," or Tim, as most know him, is a descendant of Scottish Highlanders who settled the Argyll Colony.

Tim believes that, in his lifetime, the racial harmony in the greater Fayetteville-Fort Bragg region has been better than in other areas where he has lived. Based on my perspective and experiences, I would agree.

Tim stated, "This area has become a melting pot. We have grown up together. We did not experience the civil unrest like many other areas of the country. This community is very accepting of outsiders."

We spent many sweltering backbreaking days together as youth on our *Tobacco Road,* working on his family farm or in school organizations.

"My lessons learned from growing up on a tobacco farm have been the work ethic. The principles and morals instilled in me by those experiences have been the key to my success in my life and career," Tim replied, when asked about the lessons learned from our "tobacco road" experiences.

McNeill shares the opinion that, in addition to the resilience acquired in his early lifetime and his exposure to multiculturalism, growing up in a historically rural area has given him a unique perspective.

Tim fervently expressed, "growing up in the region …has given me closeness with God and nature because I have been able to experience more of both. This is a God-fearing Christian area but it has been accepting of other religions."

Fascinating it is to note that the region encompassing communities making up the RTF are similar geographically to the former Argyll Colony.

Tim has perhaps one of the most challenging yet exhilarating jobs – overseeing the economic growth of Harnett County, the 8th fastest growing county in the *Old North State* and 75th fastest growing county in the United States. McNeill shepherds a region consisting of 11 counties and 73 municipalities. Tim believes that his upbringing has prepared him to be more resilient, thereby ready for the challenge.

"My upbringing has given me the stick-to-itiveness and the fortitude to overcome obstacles and challenges to achieve many things," the former high school Student Government Association president acknowledged.

As a result of BRAC, which, in 2005, mandated by law the closing of Fort McPherson in Atlanta and the moving of Forces Command (FORSCOM) headquarters to Fort Bragg, the Fayetteville region is expected to receive an estimated economic impact of approximately $1billion.

Unlike the way Fayetteville and Cumberland County benefited most from the economic impact of the Second World War and its aftermath, BRAC is intended to let the tentacles of planned growth and prosperity extend to the greater region at large. This is being done in a comprehensive manner, perhaps like never before in any region of North Carolina.

I share many of the aforementioned common values with McNeill and many others who reside or have resided in the Upper Cape Fear River

Valley of the Sandhills. These values were shaped by the culmination of events and relationships by a resilient people, historically multi-cultural and agrarian, i.e., close to nature. This civilian population, over numerous decades following the inception of Fort Bragg and Pope Air Force Base, melded with an even more diverse military culture, thereby gradually evolving over time. As the military is typically a more transient population, the influence of the Spirit of ArgyllAmerica still leaves its native home in the Sandhills today, traveling far and wide. Recent retirees, who continue to leave, serving their careers on other military posts in other states and abroad, often return, favoring the lifestyle they left behind.

There is promise for the future of ArgyllAmerica! Its people have spirit and are as bold as a "C-5A on a sunny, sunny day! C-5A on a sunny, sunny day!"

9

Fusion of Cultures

A man without a culture is like a grasshopper without wings.

- African Lozi Proverb

ArgyllAmerica represents the fusion between the cultures, which merged simultaneously with the fusion of the cultures. One might call it multiple fusion or multi-cultural hybridization. Let me explain further. In the Upper Cape Fear Valley, and the South in general, Africans and their descendants, often referred to as just "West Africans," were a melting pot of very distinct cultures and languages in their own right. Even today, the term polyglot is used to describe many Africans. Within the same country and region, people are often multilingual.

In the Carolinas, the descendants of Scottish Highlanders , in particular, originally Gaelic speaking people, learned to co-exist with fellow white people of England, Ireland, and Germany, among others. However, it wasn't until the early 20th century that there was a full acceptance of Scots, Irish, and Eastern Europeans as whites.

Richard Carlin, a music author, producer, and editor, and his brother, clawhammer banjoist and writer Bob Carlin, expressed very eloquently in their book *Southern Exposure: the Story of Southern Music in Pictures and Words*, what they describe as the myth that often characterizes the South.

"As powerful as the myth of the folk is the myth of the South. When we think of the southern United States, positive and negative images flood our minds: the aristocratic antebellum old South, with its southern belles and well-bred planters, versus the image of Ma and Pa Kettle, the rednecks and hillbillies who (supposedly) inhabit the southern backwoods. Cross-burning Klansmen and racial intolerance has been a sad part of the southern legacy; yet the flip side of this horrific image is the fact that blacks and whites have intermixed and mingled more strongly in the South than perhaps in any other region of the country."

Both music and dance contributed to the fusion of cultures in the American South.

The banjo, fiddle, and guitar are three instruments commonly linked when we think of folk music in the South. Among the three, the banjo is probably the most "fused" instrument, a product of a skin-stringed instrument native to West Africa and the European guitar. Because of this longstanding hybridization, the music that has resulted is a blend of African-American and European-American.

The fiddle is credited as having arrived in America along with the British, Scottish, and Irish settlers. The fiddle also contributed to providing dance music, which continued being the heart of a very fertile tradition started in their ancestral Europe.

The guitar, once considered a parlor instrument for young women during the post Civil War era, easily moved beyond being gender specific to become the most accessible, flexible, and portable of the three instruments. As the American free-enterprise system grew, with mail order and small music shops, owning a guitar became very achievable, regardless of one's socio-economic level or race.

The majority of southerners, before their move to the cities and suburbs, grew up on a Rural Free Delivery (RFD) route. This allowed them to buy banjos, fiddles, guitars, and other uncommon types of instruments economically through mail order catalogs such as Sears and Roebuck, Montgomery Ward, etc.

According to the Carlin Brothers, music often brought the races together, in particular for blacks. Whereas once considered by many late nineteenth-century white families a parlor activity or entertainment for the refined or discreet on a Sunday afternoon, music became for blacks a way of earning extra income. Because of the entrepreneurial aspect of music for blacks, it became a way of sociological uplift in the community, which allowed them to have a less formal relationship with white neighbors.

Bob Carlin strengthened his craft by working with Joe Thompson, an elderly North Carolina country fiddler. Thompson is also a common thread that influenced The Carolina Chocolate Drops (CCD).

The Carolina Chocolate Drops (CCD) were inspired by Thompson, their mentor. Thompson, a Mebane resident, happens to be African American and is a "living and breathing relic." He played a significant role in CCD being able to connect the 21st century with yesteryear. Unashamedly pure, refined, versatile, and true to their culture as "Cornbread and Butterbeans," the CCD is a refreshing modern day representation of the Spirit of ArgyllAmerica. They continue to shatter the barriers, becoming the first black band to play at Nashville's Grand Ole' Opry in 2008. The Opry's first show was in 1925. This string band, whose original musicians include Dom Flemons, Rhiannon Giddens, and Justin Robinson, understands and appreciates the origins of the folk music they play and sing. These young musicians play with their spirits free – uninhibited.

Photo: The Carolina Chocolate Drops at the Melting Point, Athens, GA

People need to understand the "why" behind lone female CCD member Rhiannon's singing of an "Acapella Gaelic Medley," rooted in the multicultural influence of Scottish Highlanders on African American slaves in the Carolinas, centuries ago.

If you close your eyes and listen to the mesmerizing, almost entrancing sounds of the CCD's "Snowden's Jig" from their Grammy Award nominated album *Genuine Negro Jig*, you might feel suspended between the spirit world and Earth. It is because of songs of expression like this with the fiddle supported by the staccato of the bones and the constant thump of the human beat box that leads Rhiannon to answer a self-imposed question that explains what they do with a response.

"Are we re-enactors or are we interpreters? I think we all feel that we are interpreters. Because we are living human beings we listen to different music. We have grown up in this world and not a world without running water. We can only bring what we have to the song," Giddens has expressed.

November 25, 1963, in Philadelphia, was a clear, cool day. Temperatures had fallen to their lowest point yet of that particular fall season. Somewhere in the City of Brotherly Love, the late Rufus Harley, "the world's first jazz bagpipe player," like millions of Americans, struggled with John F. Kennedy's senseless and untimely death. He watched on television the somber funeral services of our slain President as they took place approximately 135 miles south, down the Eastern Seaboard. On that sorrowful Monday, the Raleigh, North Carolina area-born Harley was moved by what he would later call "the spirit," wailing from the bagpipes of the Black Watch bagpipe band of the Royal Highland Regiment. Unsuccessfully, he tried to duplicate the sounds coming from the bagpipes with his saxophone. The smitted musician, not able to find bagpipes in his hometown, soon forked up $120, the money reserved for his mortgage payment, to purchase some bagpipes while on his first trip ever to New York City.

Harley, a 6' 2" talented and self taught saxophonist and flutist, embodied the Spirit of ArgyllAmerica. Wow! Fusion of cultures indeed! Imagine seeing an above average height black man, who is part African American and part Cherokee Indian, playing a bagpipe in a Scottish kilt, a dashiki, a West African kufi, or a skull cap. Eccentric, strange, fringe, left of center, worldly, global, and crazy, call him what you will. Harley did publicly state that many people actually thought he was crazy when he transitioned to the bagpipes during the 1960s and became a sideman with famous jazz musicians like John Coltrane, Dizzy Gillespie, Sonny Rollins, and numerous others.

According to his son, Messiah Patton Harley, his father might have been led to turn to the bagpipes because "...Coltrane and Rollins were smoking the sax," and were considered the preeminent saxophonists of his era. .

Rufus Harley found his cultural identity playing the bagpipes and got in touch with his soul. He once described the bagpipe and its ancient sensations as a spiritual instrument, creating the supreme sound of the planet.

"It sustains. There is a spirit that sustains us and helps us to do what we've got to do," Harley was once heard to say to an audience.

"When I'm playing it feels like I'm blowing up the Earth...All the nationalities are in the bag," Harley told his audiences, proud of not only America but the other nations, as well.

Although Harley, a high school dropout at age 16, may have lacked some formal education, he was a student of his adopted instrument. He was aware and paid proper homage to the Gaelic speaking Scottish Highlanders, perhaps knowing their many sacrifices in bringing the bagpipe to the world's forefront. Harley, being the student that he was, also knew that it was Northern Africa, particularly Egypt, where the bagpipes were thought to have originated.

I have no doubt that Dizzy Gillespie, a product of the American South and from the Sandhills area of the Carolinas heavily inhabited by the descendants of the Highland Scots, may have influenced Harley in their numerous interactions. Gillespie was very familiar with his own cultural identity and could have possibly shared his knowledge of Gaelic speaking African American descendants in his family.

Native Americans, whose numbers dwindled over time after the arrival of the European immigrants, had a lot in common with the Scottish Highlanders. The Scottish Gaels felt a kinship created by the plight of the Native American. This was evidenced by one such writing in Gaelic texts, published during the 1840s in the periodical *Cuairtear nan Gleann*, about their genocide and the hypocrisy of American imperial policy.

> *"Ann an cogadh no ann an sealgeareachd chan eil dao-*
> *ine air uachdar an t-saoghail a bheir barr air na h-Innseanaich*
> *tha tuineachadh na ceàrna sin de America nach eil air a thuin-*
> *eachadh leis na daoine geala.*

> *There is no people on the face of the earth who, in matters*
> *of war or hunting, can surpass the Indians who inhabit the region*
> *of America which is not inhabited by the white people."*

Night of Revival: A Music and Dance Celebration, as performed by the dance group

2 Near the Edge, captures the essence of ArgyllAmerica. According to Keval Kaur Khalsa, L.D. Burris, and Michael Newton, *Night of Revival* "evokes the history of two of North Carolina's communities, African-Americans and Scottish Highlanders. Although their fortunes differed greatly – Scottish Highlanders coming to America to escape oppression and Africans coming to America in the yoke of oppressed – the destiny of these two peoples became interwoven in complex and profound ways on Carolina soil. In the main region Highland settlement, the Cape Fear, several generations of African Americans spoke Gaelic and played Highland music. African-Americans affected folk tradition throughout the South, influencing musical styles, dance forms, speech patterns, food, and the rhythms of life."

This stirring, vibrant cultural performance was inspired by Jonkunnu (pronounced John Canoe), a North Carolina as well as Caribbean slave celebration, and Oidhche Challuinn, a Scottish Highland celebration.

What is there about ArgyllAmerica that connects our spirits, like tying freshly snapped tobacco leaves with "twine" around four-sided mildly splintered wooden sticks supported between two wooden hoists - each stick slightly bowed with the weight of bright green leaves, each hand full of leaves bundled and expertly joined together?

Just like the pieces of colored cloth, with their own intricate designs, sewn together by my mother's nimble fingers and her Singer® sewing machine, lives of *the folk* in the Upper Cape Fear Valley are inter-connected. Its product is the "quilting" of a people, which tells a story, not always perfect.

Fusion of Culture's purpose is not to play referee in the debate over whether what Americans have come to know as gospel music, with its call and response, is originally African or not. This debate is especially interesting to me, as I am a descendant, many generations removed, of Gaelic-speaking Africans once enslaved in the North Carolina's Cape Fear Highland settlement. I will let the empirical debate continue among the true experts and encourage that proper forums be held where the influences of the descendants of Scottish Highlanders and West Africans can be discerned.

Yale University Professor Willie Ruff, who is also a jazz musician, was correct that African-Americans spoke Gaelic, based on his research. Once a part of the famous Mitchell-Ruff Duo, Professor Ruff played and shared stages with Dizzy Gillespie, Louis Armstrong, Count Basie, and other famous musicians. He and pianist Dwike Mitchell are credited as having introduced jazz to the Soviet Union and to China.

The native Alabamian's position is said to be based on a popular anecdote where an elderly Scottish Highlander woman overheard two men speaking Gaelic as she got off the boat upon arriving in America. Upon closer inspection, the woman's expression went from excitement to horror, thinking that what she had heard about the heat and humidity of the South had turned her countrymen's skin black. Apparently, the woman actually heard two Gaelic-speaking African-Americans. Her reaction to this discovery, spoken in Gaelic with couplets and internal rhyme, was similar to the call and response we have come to know historically in the traditional black church.

'A Dhia nan Gra's

Am fa's sinn uile mar sin?'

"*Oh God of mercy, will we all become like that?*"

This is a commonly told tale that was printed and reprinted in credible books about the Scottish Highlanders in Canada, as well as in North Carolina. As a result of Ruff's work, greater interest was generated, which resulted in a documentary by BBC Scotland and even more impassioned observations in newspapers and magazines.

Dr. Newton is a leading expert on Celtic languages and culture in the Americas, and currently an assistant professor at Saint Francis Xavier University, Nova Scotia, Canada. The focus of Newton's research is Scottish Highland immigrants and their history, literature, and dance traditions. Perhaps what makes Newton unique is his work documenting the cultural interactions between Celtic peoples and descendants of Africans and indigenous people. While agreeing that Gaelic-speaking African-Americans is very factual, Newton states that the use of this particular anecdote for Gaelic psalm-singling (precenting the line) being the basis for American Negro spiritual music is unfounded. Newton, a Ph.D. in Celtic Studies from the University of Edinburgh, states that the anecdote Ruff refers to is humorous, a "migratory folklore motif" based on documented historical information spurred by the unique characteristics of the communities, as found by Gaelic-speaking immigrants.

Olly Wilson writes, in his *The Significance of the Relationship Between Afro-American and West African Music,* that he has "limited himself to a general overview of relationship of Afro-American to West African music," and encourages more detailed study. Wilson acknowledges the oversimplification that is often made when we say "African Music," noting its diversity based on individuality of cultures and ethnic groups. But he states that anyone who has a sense of music appreciation and has experienced both West African and Afro-American music should be aware of the similarities based on the scholarly work available (*Wilson, Olly. The Significance of the Relationship Between Afro-American and West African Music*).

The fusion of cultures, forced and unforced, created a multi-cultural hodge-podge we know as today's reality. Even today, among a minority of people still stuck in sins of the past, it sometimes leads to a tense environment . Yet with most others, its goodness has led to a plethora of understanding among the races and ethnicities. ArgyllAmerica is a spirit that seeks the goodness within people, thus recognizing that people are not perfect and have not traveled unblemished paths. Joel Williamson, in his book *A Rage for Order,* expresses this fusion and connectivity very vividly:

> *"Ultimately, the process was probably much more intricate than one race simply teaching the other. What we have in the*

South are two cultures in symbiosis, each constantly taking from the other, but each filtering what it takes and absorbing it relative to its special perspectives. White culture feeds off black and grows and changes, and black culture feeds from white and grows and changes. Finally, it is possible to speak of two cultures, one white and the other black, but it is also proper to speak of the fusion of cultures. This fusion, which occurred in the last three decades of slavery, forms the substratum that joins black and white today – it is the substantial beginning of the oneness of modern Southern life. It is why black people and white people in similar situations perform very much alike. It is why they share many of the same values. It is why they can, if need be, sometimes relate to one another with great intensity and understanding."

ArgyllAmerica is the world as I know it. It is that which has swayed me and millions of others, now and before me. As stated in the introduction, the Spirit of ArgyllAmerica is inclusive, not bound to one person or to one race or culture. Transgenerational and portable, the Spirit of ArgyllAmerica has influenced the uniqueness of the American South, thereby creating its own popular culture.

Similarly, to most southerners, it is welcoming, not limiting. Like the southeasterly flowing blackwaters of North Carolina's Cape Fear River, birthed where the Haw and the Deep Rivers meet, its spirit has defied a revolution, a civil war, world wars, and racial and civil conflict.

The Spirit of ArgyllAmerica does not belong to me, alone. Quite "au contraire" – it is shared. Sure, I have attempted to capture the aura or the essence of what numerous people have felt through the years – the pursuit of racial harmony, resiliency of the people and their sustainability (the connection to nature). North Carolina native son, author, and playwright Paul Green both felt and experienced aspects of it and thus directly and sometimes indirectly expressed it in his work. In Green's era, "it," i.e., ArgyllAmerica was not defined as such. Nevertheless, once readers gain familiarity with his work, the connection is imminent. It is apparent that the Pulitzer Prize winning Green, a man ahead of his generation, socially and culturally, lived, tasted and felt the fusion of cultures he experienced in eastern North Carolina. It was a natural environment, providing stimuli from the tea-colored waters of the Cape Fear, the undulating topography of the Sandhills, and the once-threatened but now revived longleaf pine.

An artist, after creating the conceptual sketch and having selected the various paints and supplies, develops the subject matter. When finished and legally duplicated, it is eventually showcased as a print lying beneath a glass pane. It is the framing and matting which has been selected that gives it character, support, and distinction. So it is with the people whose spirits embody ArgyllAmerica's principles or core values. Your concept of ArgyllAmerica though unique, may very well have the same principles, only matted and framed differently.

"Whom does the ArgyllAmerica in you belong to?"

Lastly, to further revise the famed curiosity of the Scottish Highlanders of yesteryear, ask, "Where does your ArgyllAmerica come from?"

Epilogue

A man without a culture is like a grasshopper without wings.

- African Lozi Proverb

L iving in the Spirit of ArgyllAmerica means being resilient. It also means, as my forefathers and the descendants of Scottish Highlanders and Native Americans did, discovering the sustainable connection between God and nature.

My siblings and I didn't realize it as children growing up in the rural Sandhills of North Carolina, but Mom and Dad unknowingly delved into organic farming from time to time. They probably didn't think of using dried manure obtained from the chicken coop or hog pen on vegetables in the garden as organic farming.

Mom, Dad, and other resilient kinfolks and neighbors seemed happiest when they were tilling the soil, planting seeds or seedlings, and reaping their harvest.

In retrospect, they were a lot smarter than I. They had the benefit of knowledge transferred to them not only from our ancestors here in America but from people, probably subsistent farmers, natives of West Central Africa's Cameroon and Equatorial Guinea.

Let me be clear, I am not suggesting that sophisticated urban and suburban dwellers break city and county codes and put chicken coops and hog pens in back yards. This is not a call to action for the hogs and chickens. Fortunately, lessons can be learned by understanding the reasons some do what they do.

The future of ArgyllAmerica is definitely the fusion of ethnicities, along with the existing races and cultures. With the tremendous migration of Latinos in the Southeastern United States and, especially, historically stable employment states like North Carolina and Georgia, they are positioned to influence and embrace common values.

According to the late Dr. John Hope Franklin, distinguished professor, author, and historian, "It is so difficult for our country to establish and maintain communities that have a healthy mix of white Americans, African Americans, Asians, Latinos, and other groups that are an essential part of the American landscape."

Intuitively, Franklin's book *The Color Line* also gives us our path forward in pursuing racial harmony. Although referring to blacks and whites, his message is not limited to them. His words resonate powerfully, telling Americans the following:

> *"Perhaps the very first thing we need to do as a nation and as individual members of society is to confront our past and see it for what it is. It is a past filled with some of the ugliest possible examples of racial brutality and degradation in human history. We need to recognize it for what it was and is and not explain it away, excuse it, or justify it. Having done that, we should then make a good-faith effort to turn our history around so that we can see it in front of us, so that we can avoid doing what we have done for so long. If we do that, whites will discover that African Americans possess the same human qualities that other Americans possess, and African Americans will discover that white Americans are capable of the most sublime expressions of human conduct of which all human beings are capable. Then, we need to do everything possible to emphasize the positive qualities that all of us have, qualities which we have never utilized to the fullest, but*

which we must utilize if we are to solve the problem of the color line in the twenty-first century."

Maybe you've seen multi-talented bass singer, actor, activist, and athlete Paul Roberson's moving rendition of "The House I Live In" *(What is America to Me)* – on video, of course. Roberson, perhaps one the greatest Americans in the 20th century, spent much of his early life seeking civil and racial justice – mostly ending up frustrated.

You are definitely getting up in age if you were witness to New Orleans-born Mahalia Jackson and her soulful rendition of "The House I Live In." Like Roberson, she grew up in the Jim Crow era, seeking but not fully experiencing the desires expressed in the song.

Neill Diamond, a son of descendants of Polish and Russian Jews and known as the writer of the Monkees' famous hit "I'm a Believer," "Sweet Caroline," and other famous songs, sang an inspiring "The House I Live In" as a duet with Frank Sinatra.

Other notables like Sonny Rollins and Josh White sang "The House I Live In." Perhaps you heard the soulful R&B singer, Patti LaBelle's rendition of "The 'House I Live In," as she serenaded Frank "Old Blue Eyes" Sinatra on his 80th birthday in April 2007. As often, her performance brought her a standing ovation.

But it was Frank Sinatra who started it all with his1945 rendition; he also starred in the short film with the same name. Sinatra, a descendant of Italian American parents, himself had been a victim of discrimination.

"What is America to me?
A name, a map, or a flag I see;
A certain word, democracy.
What is America to me?

The house I live in,
A plot of earth, a street,
The grocer and the butcher,
Or the people that I meet;

The children in the playground,
The faces that I see,
All races and religions,
That's America to me…"
(Abel Meeropol aka Lewis Allan & Earl Robinson)

Yes indeed! The ArgyllAmerica I know is not just a place. It is also a spirit, embodying the fusion of cultures that reflects "the house I live in," which continuously, and always striving, is the spirit I seek.

Largo vive el Espiritud de ArgyllAmerica!
(Long live the Spirit of ArgyllAmerica!)

ABOUT THE AUTHOR

Born in Sanford, North Carolina, Ernest Gilchrist was raised in the rural Sandhills of nearby western Harnett County, minutes from Fayetteville-Fort Bragg. There, he was exposed to unique multicultural relationships, which would influence, shape and mold him.

Gilchrist grew up from childhood with a fascination for journalism and the literary arts. While in high school he served as a sports editor of the yearbook and school newspaper.

At Campbell University, he would later study under English professor and renowned poet, Dr. Shelby Stephenson, past winner of the North Carolina Award for literature, the highest civilian award given in the Tar Heel State.

In addition to a bachelor's degree in Business Administration from the university in "The Creek", Gilchrist holds a MBA in International Business with a concentration in marketing from Mercer University's Eugene Stetson School of Business and Economics.

Although having spent over half his life living in metropolitan Atlanta, in his book, *Fusion of Cultures: The Spirit of ArgyllAmerica™ Revealed* he has "come home" to his rural roots with an urban consciousness. Gilchrist is "Hotlanta" smooth with Carolina fried green tomatoes charm.

Gilchrist's career has taken him appreciatively to numerous states and industries, working in a variety of management and consulting capacities over several decades.

Recently, he founded BRANDideas, LLC, a branding creation, development and implementation organization. Its first intellectual property, ArgyllAmerica™ , derived from the former Argyll Colony in America, is a cultural brand that was the genesis for writing the book.

Gilchrist gave a talk at the first annual Celts in the Americas Conference in Antigonish, Nova Scotia Canada in 2011 on multiculturalism among descendants of Scottish Highlanders, descendants of Gaelic speaking African-Americans and Native Americans in North Carolina's Upper Cape Fear River Valley.

He is married to the former Synetha Ann Bennett of Montgomery, Alabama and have two young adult "kids", Darius and Tamara.

ABOUT THE COVER DESIGNER
Michael Angelo Chester

Born in Columbus, Georgia and raised in Detroit, Michigan, Michael is a "visualist" whose career spans several visual media, including fine art, graphic art, still photography and film/video. Michael obtained his degree in graphic arts from The Computer Arts Institute in San Francisco. He has designed CD covers, books, logos, and magazine ads for several clients including performers Public Enemy, Lenny Williams, and has designed the books *Naturally Yours Cookbook* and Moore Black Press Publishing.

Michael is also a professional portrait artist whose clients includes Anita Baker, Georgia State Senator Emmanuel Jones, former Atlanta Mayor Sam Massell and Chick-fil-A founder and CEO, S. Truett Cathy.

"It has been a real eye-opening and learning experience working with Ernest. I would recommend it for all Americans."

Facebook: Michael Angelo Chester

michaelangelochester@gmail.com

www.michaelangelochester.com

REFERENCES

Avery, L.G. (1994). (Ed.) A Southern Life: Letters of Paul Green, 1916-1981, edited by Laurence G. Avery, The University of North Carolina Press, Chapel Hill and London.

Avery, L.G. (1998). (Ed.) A Paul Green Reader, edited with an introduction by Laurence G. Avery, The University of North Carolina Press, Chapel Hill and London.

Aymemi, A. (Father). (1942). The Bubis on Fernando Po (Los Bubis en Fernando Poo), a collection of articles published in the colonial journal Spanish Guinea, Publication sponsored by Juan Fontán y Lobé and financed by the Office of Morocco and Colonies, 1942. Translation by ColHerbertn Truelsen, 2003. Retrieved in 2009 from http://www.thebubis.com.

Bauer, M. D. (2008, Fall). "Call me Paul": the long, hot summer of Paul Green and Richard Wright. Mississippi Quarterly. Retrieved on March 28, 2010 from http://findarticles.com/p/articles/mi.

Belt, N. (1989). Story of the Quilt Square: Cameron Hill Fire Tower. Retrieved on May 14, 2009 from http://www.harnett.org.

Bethune, L.E. (2002 – 2007). Lawrence E. Bethune's M.U.S.I.C.s Project (Musical*Unique*Scottish*Identifiable* Charact eristic): A Dissertation Tracing Scottish Folk Music from

18th Century Scotland to Colonial Carolina through a system analyzing and categorizing melodic phrases called MUSICs. Unpublished doctoral dissertation presented in partial fulfillment of the Requirements for the Degree of Philosophy by Research from the School of Applied Arts of the University of Strathclyde, Glasgow. Retrieved from http://www.dalhousielodge.org/Thesis/scotstonc.htm on December 5, 2006.

Boyd, J. (Copyright 1925). Drums. Charles Scribner's Sons. Renewal copyright 1953 by Katherine Boyd; with pictures by N.C. Wyeth. Illustrations copyright 1928 Charles Scribner's Sons; Renewal copyright 1928. Reset March 1965.

Brown, G. S. (1962, September 10). The Southern Resort of a Proper Bostonian, Sports Illustrated. Retrieved from http://sportsillustrated.cnn.com/vault/article/magazine/MAG1135063/2/index.html.

Burnes, C. (1977, March 12). Texas Southern, Camels Collide, The Kansas City Times.

Camels Are No. 2 In Nation! (1977, March 15). Creek Pebbles, VIII (19).

Camels Win. (1977, March 3). The Raleigh Times.

Campbell University - University Report, 2009-2010.

Carlin, R., Carlin, R. (2000). Southern Exposure: the Story of Southern Music in Pictures and Words. Watson-Guptill

Publications. New York.

Carolina Chocolate Drops (CCD). (2009, December 16). Genuine Negro Jig. Preview by Nonesuch Records with Joe Henry, Producer.

Carolina In My Mind Lyrics. (n.d.). Retrieved on November 12, 2009 from http://www.elyrics.net/read/j/james-taylor-lyrics/carolina-in-my-mind-lyrics.html.

Carr, A.J. (1977, March 10). Camel Defensive Scheme Waylays NAIA Foe, 71-56. The News and Observer.

Carr, A.J. (1977, March 14). Camels' Big Week: A Boom and A Bust. The News and Observer.

Chaney, J. (1976, November). Camel outlook: Wait-and see. Fayetteville Times.

Church, R.J. H., Clarke, J., Clarke, P.J.H., Henderson, .J.R. (1964). Africa and the Islands. New York: John Wiley & Sons, Inc.

CIA-the World Fact Book – Equatorial Guinea. Retrieved on March 29, 2009 from https://www.cia.gov/library/publications/the-world-factbook/geos/ek.html.

Collins, Lt. Colonel William. Interview Regarding the United States Military, May 2010.

Common Scottish Gaelic. (n.d.). Retrieved on February 25, 2010 from http://www.savegaelic.org).

Ernest R. Gilchrist

Common Scottish Gaelic. (n.d.). Retrieved on June 7, 2011 from
    http://www.savegaelic.org.

Curtin, P. D. (1969). The Atlantic Slave Trade: A Census.
    Madison, The University of Wisconsin Press.

Dauner, J. T. (1977, March 12). Kansas Blizzard Sweeps Gentle
    Rain into Area:Rain Soaks Two States. The Kansas City
    Times. 109(160).

DeVane, S. Biblical Recorder. (2008, September 8). Football
    Returns to Campbell University. Retrieved on October 11,
    2009 from www.biblicalrecorder.com.

Doyle, D. H. (2001). Faulkner's County: The Historical Roots of
    Yoknapatawpha. The University of North Carolina Press:
    Chapel Hill and London.

Doyles New York. (n.d.). Dogs in Art. Retrieved from
    www.doylenewyork.com in 2010.

Earley, Lawrence S. (2004). Looking for Longleaf: The Fall and Rise
    of an American Forest. The University of North Carolina
    Press: Chapel Hill and London. Equatorial Guinea: the
    Land, Relief, Drainage and Soils. (n.d.). Encyclopedia
    Brittanica. Retrieved in 2009 from
    http://wf2dnvr16.webfeat.org.

Fennelly, Martin. (2007, May 7). State vs. Maryland Was One
    for Ages. Retrieved from Tampa Bay Online (TBO.com)
    on September 13, 2009.

Fowler, Malcolm. (1955). They Passed This Way: A Personal Narrative of Harnett County History. Centennial Edition, Harnett County Centennial, Inc.

Franklin, John Hope. (1963). The Emancipation Proclamation. Doubleday & Company, Inc. New York.

From Staff and Wire Reports. (1977, March 11). Unseeded Camels Reach Semifinal In NAIA. The Fayetteville Observer.

Gantz, C. O. (2005). Discovering the Forest: Sandhills Forest Life in North and South Carolina. iUniverse, Inc., Lincoln.

Gates, H. L., Jr. (2006). African American Lives, PBC Documentary.

Godwin, D. (1990, February 21). Harnett Man, 95, Recalls Life, Including Working for Rockefellers and Others. The Sanford Herald, Volume (70)(45).

Gomez, M. A. (1998). Exchanging Our Country Marks: The Transformation of African Identities In the Colonial And Antebellum South. The University of North Carolina Press, Chapel Hill and London.

Green, P. (1970). Home to My Valley. The University of North Carolina Press, Chapel Hill.

Green, P.E. (May, 1996). North Carolina English Teacher. (23). Spring Issue.

Guinea Equatorial. (n.d.). Retrieved from http://www.republi

cofequitorialguinea.net/About/indes.cfm on March 30, 2009.

Haley, A. (1976). Roots: Saga of an American Family. Dell Publishing Co., Inc.

Hansen, H. (1941). Louisiana: A Guide to the State. Hastings House Publishing, New York.

Hard work pays off: Campbell grads get diplomas, advice. (2010, May 16). The Fayetteville Observer, CXCIV – No. 238.

Hevesi, D. (2006, August 13). Rufus Harley, 70, Dies; Adapted Bagpipes to Jazz. The New York Times. Retrieved on July 24, 2010 from www.nytimes.com.

Hight, R.V. et al. (1977). Campbell College Men's Basketball Media Guide (1977-1978), Highland Printers.

Hodges, B. (1971, February 7). Book Nook. Durham Morning Herald.

Howells, W. D. (1964). The Rise of Silas Lapham. First Published 1985, Cornwall Press: Introductory Copyright, by Dodd, Mead & Company, Inc.

Hurmence, B. (1984, 1986). My Folks Don't Want Me To Talk About Slavery. John F. Blair Publisher, Winston-Salem, North Carolina.

Hyre, K. Interview Regarding the Weymouth Woods State Preserve and the James Boyd House, January 29, 2010.

Irwin, J. D., O'Shea, K. (2008). Overhills: The Images of America. Arcadia Publishing.

Ivy, T. P. (1923). The Long Leaf Pine: With Prefatory Remarks On the Political and Geological History of North Carolina and the Sandhills. The Sandhill Citizen Print (Foss & Morris). Southern Pines, NC.

Jackson, J. M. (1998). My Life: Lies and Misinformation. Unpublished Family Documents.

Jackson, J. Telephone Interview Regarding the Life of Isaac Brinkley Clark, May 24, 2009.

Jenifer, P. (1977, February 20) Methodist Turns On Camels, 61-57. The Fayetteville Observer-Times.

Jenifer, P. (1977, March 14). Welcome. Fayetteville Times.

Jenifer, P. (1977, March 14). Where It Begins. Fayetteville Times.

Johnson, W. A. Interview Regarding the Life of Paul Green and Relatives, September 24, 2010.

Lyndon Baines Johnson Library and Museum: The President's Daily diary: April 6, 1968. Retrieved October 11, 2009 from http://www.lbjlib.utexas.edu/johnson/archives.hom/ Diary/1968/680406.asp.

McNeill, T. Interview Regarding the Values Obtained Growing Up in the Upper Cape Fear River Valley, April 23, 2011.

McWhitney, G. (1988). Cracker Culture: Celtic Ways in the Old South. The University of Alabama Press, Tuscaloosa and London.

Menzer, Joe, Four Corners: How UNC, N.C. State, Duke and Wake Forest Made North Carolina the Center of the Basketball Universe, Simon & Schuster, 1999.

Meuller, R. (1989). Air Force Bases, (1), Active Air Force Bases Within the United States. Washington, D.C.: Office of Air Force History, United States Air Force.

Meyer, D. (1957, 1961). The Highland Scots of North Carolina 1732-1776, The University of North Carolina Press – Chapel Hill.

Millegan, K., Sutton, A., Rogers, T., Chaitkin, A., Hopsicker, D., Webster, T. et al. (2003). Fleshing Out Skull & Bones: Investigations into America's Powerful Most Secret Society. Trine Day.

Miller, M. (1974). Plain Speaking: An Oral Biography of Harry S. Truman. Putnam, New York.

Montgomery, A. (2006, July). Village of Pinehurst Historic District Standards and Guidelines.

Moskos, C.C., Butler, J. S. (1996). All That We Can Be: Black Leadership and Racial Integration the Army Way, Basic Books, A division of Harper Collins Publishers, Inc.

Murdock, S. D. (Copyright 1998). The Influences of Aircraft Development on Runway Design. (From a report submit ted to Embry-Riddle Aeronautical University in 1995). Retrieved from http://www.airforcebase.net/usaf/runways.html.

Nasser, H.E. (2008). U.S. Hispanic Population to Triple by 2050. USA Today. Retrieved on July 19, 2010 from http://www.usatoday.com/news/nation/2008.

Newton, M. (2010, June). Did you hear about the Gaelic-speaking African?: Scottish Gaelic Folklore about Identity in North America. Comparative Studies, 8(2), 00-00.

Newton, M. (October, 2001) We're Indians Sure Enough: the Legacy of the Scottish Highlanders in the United States. Saorsa Media.

Page, H.F. (1934). Lyrics and Legends of the Cape Fear Country. Unknown publisher.

Pearce, J. W. (1976). Campbell College: Big Miracle at Little Buies Creek, 1887-1974. Nashville: Broadman Press.

Percy A. Rockefeller Weds Miss Stillman. (1901, April 24). New York Times. Retrieved from the http://www.nytimes.com/.

Poole, S. M. (2004, July 23). Test Details Ex-Mayor's African Ties: Young Traces Bloodline to Sierra Leone. The (GA) Atlanta Journal-Constitution, page A3.

Powell, W.S. (Ed.). (1968). The North Carolina Gazetteer: A Dictionary of Tar Heel Places. Chapel Hill: University of North Carolina Press, 1968.

Ramsey, J. (2009, February 5). Rockefeller Home in Overhills Burns. Fayetteville Observer. Retrieved on February 5, 2009 from www.fayobserver.com.

Ray, C. (2001, March). Highland Heritage: Scottish Americans in the American South. The University of North Carolina Press.

Roberts, Camels Gain More Focus. (1977, March 11). The Fayetteville Observer.

Roper, J.H. (2003). Paul Green: Playwright of the Real South. The University of Georgia Press, Athens, Georgia.

Sandhills History – A Storied Past. Retrieved on December 13, 2009 from http://www.sandhillsgolf.com/sandhillshistory.html.

Simpson, C.M., III. (1983). Inside the Green Berets: The First Thirty Years. Presido Press, Navato, California.

Siskel, G. (1998). Thumbs Up for Jordan: Gene Siskel Rates Michael Jordan's Best Performance in New York. Retrieved from http://www.nba.com/jordan/siskelonmj.html.

Sprunt, J. (1914). Chronicles of the Cape Fear River. Edwards and Broughton Printing Company, Raleigh, North Carolina.

Stewart, Dr. H.D. A Brief History of the Kirkin'. Retrieved from http://calpresbyterian.org/History/KirkinOfTheTartan.html on August 6, 2010.

Sundiata, I.K. (1996). The Bight of Biafra and Fernando Po in the Era of Abolition, 1827-1930. The University of Wisconsin Press.

The Alan Mason Chesney Medical Archives of the Johns Hopkins Medical Institutions. American Clinical and Climatological Association. Retrieved on December 12, 2009 from http://www.medicalarchives.jhmi.edu/climatologicalassocia tion.html.

Third Crisis. (1934, September 27). Creek Pebbles, p. 1

Thompson, L. (1988). The All Americans: The 82nd Airborne. David & Charles Publishers, United Kingdom, Distributed in U.S.A. by Sterling Publishing Co., Inc. New York, N.Y.

Tuck, W. P. (Ed.). (1986). A Mosiac of Memories of Campbell University, 1987-1987. Photocopied by Service Entereprises, Campbell University, Buies Creek, NC.

Tuck, W.P. (Ed.). (1992). A Mosiac of Memories of Leslie Hartwell Campbell, 1892-1970. Published by A.P. Gamma Mu Project, Campbell University, Buies Creek, NC.

UNC Center for Civil Rights Civil Rights. (2006, August 25). Invisible Fences: Municipal Underbounding in Southern Moore County. Retrieved from http://www.lcrm.lib.unc. edu/voice/works/w/invisible-fences/s/1 on December 28, 2008.

Wallace, Dr. J. Telephone Interview Regarding President Jerry

Ernest R. Gilchrist

Wallace's Life and Tenure at Campbell University, March 2, 2011.

Welcome to the Highlands, Gaelic in America. (n.d.). Retrieved from http://www.calumandcatriona.com in December 29, 2006.

Williamson, J. (1986). A Rage for Order: Black/White Relations in the American South Since Emancipation, Oxford University Press, New York.

Wilson, Jr., O. (1974). The Significance of the Relationship Between Afro-American and West African Music, The Black Perspective in Music. Retrieved from http://negroartist.com/music.

Witzel, M. (2005). The Encylopedia of the History of American Management, Edingburgh: Printed by Thomas and Archibald Constable.

Wynn, N. A. (2010). The African American Experience during World War II. Rowman & Littlefield Publishers, Inc., Lanham, Maryland.

Index

Ernest R. Gilchrist

CPSIA information can be obtained
at www.ICGtesting.com
Printed in the USA
FSHW010311170621
82415FS

9 780615 519609